I0457831

ANSWER TO ANXIOUS

A Student's Guide to Resolving Test-Taking,
Performance, and Social Anxiety

JAMES TREADWAY

www.growthwise.us

Copyright © 2025 James Treadway

All Rights Reserved
No portion of this book may be reproduced mechanically, electronically, or by any other means, including photocopying, without securing the advanced written permission of the author. Likewise, no portion of this book may be posted to a website or distributed by any other means without securing the advanced written permission of the author.

Limits of Liability and Disclaimer of Warranty
This book is strictly for informational and educational purposes only. Neither the author nor the publisher shall be liable for any misuse of the enclosed material. The author and the publisher do not guarantee that anyone following these techniques, suggestions, tips, ideas, or strategies will be successful or healed. The author and the publisher shall have neither liability nor responsibility to anyone with respect to any loss or damage caused, or alleged to be caused, directly or indirectly, by the information or suggestions contained in this book.

Medical Disclaimer
To the extent that any medical or health information is shared in this book, it is provided as an information resource only and is not to be used or relied on for any diagnostic or treatment purposes. Any such information is not intended to be patient information, does not create any patient-physician relationship, and should not be used as a substitute for professional diagnosis and treatment.

Published by Made to Change the World™ Publishing
Nashville, Tennessee

ISBN: 978-1-956837-57-5 (print)
ISBN: 978-1-956837-58-2 (ebook)

Printed globally.

Dedication

If you doubt yourself and feel powerless to perform under pressure, this book is for you.

Maybe you haven't yet learned how to let your brilliance flow, but it *is* inside you, waiting to come out.

Read on. You've got this, more than you know.

Contents

There's a spectrum that defines how you show up to anything in life, and it's marked by two opposite energies: "play with" versus "succeed at." "Play with" is joyous, relaxed, and spontaneous, while "succeed at" is driven, intense, and persistent. Both energies are great! Problems arise when you fall too far out of balance towards one energy or the other. If you're experiencing performance anxiety, then you've dipped too far into "succeed at" energy, and the results that come next are entirely predictable. They'll describe what you've been experiencing exactly.

The sweet spot of your peak performance, be it on tests, in sports or the performing arts, or even in socializing, happens when you find the healthy balance between "play with" and "succeed at." We call this sweet spot in the middle "Flow." Life, and your gifts, flow brilliantly when you're in this place. This chapter paints a picture of what it's like to come back from too much "succeed at" and to return to the healthy balance between "play with" and "succeed at."

CHAPTER 3: Know Your Nervous System. 51

To ground yourself deeper in flow, get to know your nervous system, made up of your brain, spinal cord, and the nerves throughout the body. Together, they run your entire body. At any moment of the day, your nervous system is moving towards a sympathetic or parasympathetic response to life. In sympathetic, you're becoming more stressed and anxious, while in parasympathetic, you're becoming more calm and grounded. Accessing parasympathetic in any moment is critical to escaping the stress vortex of performance anxiety.

CHAPTER 4: Find Flow in Parasympathetic 65

Get yourself into flow and parasympathetic with three easy moves that you can do anytime, while nobody knows you're doing them.

CHAPTER 5: Performing in Flow!. 79

To see how different it is to perform in flow, imagine you're a student who used to have test anxiety. You used to physically tense up and tell yourself terrifying stories about how incapable you were. But you're different, now. You've read the first four chapters of this book, and you're ready to answer to anxious. Studying and test-taking proceed very differently as you keep yourself from falling too far into "succeed at" and stay in a parasympathetic flow throughout.

CHAPTER 6: Heal the Root Causes of Your Anxiety 87

Anything you're feeling in this moment that doesn't feel like love—such as anxiety, anger, sadness, resentment, boredom, etc.—has its roots in emotional wounds that you've experienced in the past. The secret to healing these wounds, so that these feelings don't get continuously reactivated in your life, is to bring them love. Love heals. Be the loving adult to the hurt emotions you have inside, and gradually over time, you'll find yourself no longer feeling the triggers that used to throw you into anxiety, anger, sadness, etc. This is actually the path to enlightenment that spiritual masters like Michael Singer, Byron Katie, Eckhart Tolle and many others describe in their books and talks.

Foreword

by Dan Lerman

In life, each of us is the star of our own movie. So why are we so damn anxious about performing? It's our movie, after all!

Can't we just show up the way we want to?

The answer, it turns out, is trickier than it sounds. And the topic—performance anxiety—is more relevant than ever. In an age where even toddlers are being prepped for college, we've made pressure inescapable.

Today's youth are growing up in what Jonathan Haidt calls The Anxious Generation: bombarded by comparisons, addicted to feedback, and terrified to fail.

We've told them that life is one long audition, and we wonder why they freeze.

For the past two decades I've been a teacher and tutor to thousands of high achievers from the world's best schools, and today I see more students struggling with test anxiety, and general everyday anxiety, than ever before. Hard work and brilliance don't help if your nerves prevent you from accessing them when it counts.

I met James years ago while interviewing tutors to join me in teaching a summer ACT boot camp. I rented a tiny West Village office in New York City and asked eleven applicants to "teach me something—anything."

Some walked me through math problems. Others explained photosynthesis. James? He exploded into the room like he was on Broadway. He got me and my colleague out of our seats, made us dance around, and within minutes transformed the space with his presence, humor, and playful wisdom. He was easily our first choice.

Since then, James has become a friend and one of my first calls when life feels like it's buckling. I've called him when I felt burned out, was chasing something big, or my stomach turned in knots before a talk. He always picks up, and he always knows what to say.

James is truly one of one. What sets James apart is a relentless commitment to living "the work." He's invested two decades and over a million dollars into masterminds, seminars, and world-class coaching, ultimately transforming a lifelong personal pursuit of growth into something he can share with the rest of us.

This book is that gift. It's a system, a mindset, and a mirror for where you are if performance anxiety has been a problem, as it has for so many of us. James walks you to the root causes of your anxiety (cognitive, emotional, nervous system-level) and hands you tools that *work*. I use them myself and share them with my students.

I hope this book means as much to you as it does to me.

I hope, in reading it, you get to feel what I felt the first time I met James: that spark. That shift. That sense that you are finally free to play your own damn part!

You've got this!

Dan Lerman

Dan Lerman is a professor of Cognitive Science, Psychology, and Human Development at Columbia University. He founded the Professional Tutoring Program at Columbia and is the Director of The League of Extraordinary Tutors.

Acknowledgments

First, to my parents—thank you for the perfect mix of drive, honesty, and ever-committed, unflinching love that you gave me; plus all the unintended insecurity and pain that's given purpose to my life: healing the alienation we feel as people, in ourselves and with each other. Man, do I love this purpose. I cannot be grateful enough for how patient, flexible, and accepting you two have been of my outside-the-box choices, railings against your parenting, and extreme passion for all I pursue—all of which has been a lot for you to deal with!

I feel so blessed that I get to show up to you now from the other side of the anxiety I used to suffer. It held me back in my relationship with you as much as it did in the rest of my life. We have so much love and fun to enjoy now going forward.

Second, to the phenomenal teachers who've infused my life with so much insight, love, and courage—thank you, thank you, thank you: Tony Robbins, Alison Armstrong (from whom I first heard "play with" versus "succeed at"!), Greg Paul, Father Gregory Boyle, Chris Voss, Julie King, Haim Ginott, Adele Faber and Elaine Mazlish, Harvill Hendrix and Helen LaKelly Hunt, Marie Kondo, Priya Narthakii, the HeartMath Institute, John Sarno, Michael Singer, James Redfield, Andrea Waltz and Richard Fenton, Ken Page, Paolo Coelho, Abe Wald, Alice Miller, Taita Juanito, Gerry Powell, and last but the very opposite of least, Grandmother Aya.

Third, to my wonderful illustrator Angela Chiang—thank you for the patience and talent that you brought to this book!

Introduction

"We were told you had a different approach. You were very unique in how you teach the tests, and you got consistently strong results across different sets of students. You were the person to go to. And then my daughter came down and exclaimed one night, 'Oh God, what James taught me really works!'"

—Karen, parent of a formerly anxious test taker

"[In the audition], I learned to focus all of my energy into joy instead of wasting my energy on a few little things that could go wrong. I messed up terribly in one part, but all of my other stuff was pretty much how I wanted it to be, and I still got in. Now I can truly believe, rather than just trying to convince myself, that mistakes ACTUALLY ARE ok, because I still got in. I'm sure my auditions in the future will be even better as long as I play for fun, and accept that mistakes will happen. I'm finally grasping the idea of "play with" energy, as I still had some nerves, but only a small amount that did not affect my performance!"

—Sam, formerly anxious flutist

Test anxiety, performance anxiety, social anxiety: you must have one of these if you're reading this book.

Maybe you're a high schooler preparing for the SAT or ACT.

Or a 7th grader who blanks out on his math tests.

Maybe you're applying to graduate school and have to take the LSAT, GMAT, or any of the other graduate school entrance exams.

Maybe you're an athlete—a volleyball player who just can't find her game anymore. Your coach has a bad habit of yelling at you and your teammates, and you're terrified of making mistakes now. The game you used to love is one you now secretly fantasize about quitting.

Maybe you're a musician trying out for your city's elite high school symphony, and for some reason, you just can't get past the belief that you need to be *perfect* at your audition in order to be accepted. The pressure of that expectation makes you tremble, and now you screw up songs that you used to play easily.

Or is it social anxiety that wreaks havoc on you? You don't know what to say so you clam up in interactions, become tight and awkward, and then walk away from the other person feeling like you've just failed the conversation. And you don't know how to stop!

Man, these situations are painful, and you might have experienced more than one of them.

Well guess what—each of the people described above is a person I've worked with who's broken free from the anxiety that held them back. They've all gone on to flourish. They found their flow, and you can, too.

You can ace the test and show your natural intelligence.

You can compete in the sport you love, or perform the art you've spent so much time mastering, and simply let your gifts shine.

You can be dropped into a party full of people you don't know and genuinely connect with anyone.

To get there, read this book to the end. I made it short because I wanted to get straight to the point with the approaches that have changed my life and the lives of my clients.

So why listen to me about performance anxiety? I am a Harvard graduate (as a Harvard graduate, I must tell you this) who scored a 1520 on his SAT and 1550 on his GRE, was captain and MVP of the soccer team in high school, and founded a leading boutique tutoring company in his adult life.

But Harvard, high test scores, and athletic and business success have nothing to do with why you should listen to me about performance anxiety.

You should listen to me because anxiety has been a stumbling block my entire life, and I finally solved it not just for myself, but for hundreds of clients in test taking, socializing, athletics, and the performing arts.

Above all, it was crippling social anxiety that forced me to get to the bottom of this, developing the skills that my clients now rave about.

When I was eleven years old, I entered middle school and started to doubt my ability to talk to people. With five elementary schools in my town merging into one middle school, and puberty creeping around the corner, my peers and I began to feel incredibly insecure, and social life devolved into a ferocious popularity contest.

Somehow we all knew that a certain classmate—I'll call him Brandon—going to be the most popular kid in sixth grade. He was funny, brash, occasionally mean, and good at sports. Brandon would be king. We just knew it.

In the first days of sixth grade, Brandon and his friends walked up to me between classes and asked, "What's up? What are you up to?" I stammered, not knowing what to say, and told them, "I'm going to band," before tightly walking on to music class.

That was it, my audition for popularity and membership in Brandon's friend group, and I'd failed pathetically. I was never going to be popular.

The experience sounds childish, except that nerve-racking fear in conversations continued for the next twenty-five years. I wasn't sure what to say to people. I felt petrified that they were judging me as inadequate or weird, and that whatever I said next was going to be judged as well—another social mistake that I could not stop making.

As a conversation continued, I'd become more and more uptight, until finally I knew that the other person could tell how uptight and strange I was acting. When the conversation ended, I'd walk away feeling like a failure. For years this happened, devastating my confidence and ability to make friends.

What was wrong with me? Why couldn't I do this? Wasn't talking to people supposed to be easy?

Over time, I became more anxious and depressed, and at times in my twenties, I wasn't sure I wanted to be alive. I would stand on subway platforms in Boston or New York where I lived, and when the train came, I made sure to stand behind a column or walk in the opposite direction, because I was afraid that the part of me that wanted to throw myself in front of the train was going to win the argument.

Once I began working and earning money at age twenty, I invested all of it into workshops, seminars, retreats, and books that might give me the answers I craved to find: how to stop feeling so anxious, insecure, and unsuccessful at connecting with people. I looked for answers like someone with their head on fire looks for water. I probably invested $1.5 million in this pursuit—everything I earned in my twenties and thirties.

Thankfully, I found the answers I needed. Today, I can drop into *any* social context and converse easily and genuinely with people. Connecting feels easy, a joy, and something I'm actually good at.

My everyday anxiety, which was tested by a neurofeedback clinician during my mid-twenties to be three standard deviations above the mean (ninety-ninth percentile!), feels completely calmed and relaxed now.

Meanwhile, the tools I've been researching and experimenting with around my own anxiety have proven to be exceptionally effective with my students in *all* areas of performance anxiety: social, academic, athletic, and performing (musicians, actors, etc.).

If test-taking brought you to this book, I'll share something annoying: I was blessed with barely any test-taking anxiety in my life. For tests, I somehow had the perfect mindset: I'd work extremely hard, not worry about mistakes, trust it was all going to work out in the end, and keep going after my goal score until I got a really good result (which didn't need to be perfect).

If only I'd known to approach the rest of my life that way! Because that's the formula right there. But because that paragraph won't do it, I'll spell out the success formula across the rest of this short book.

You'll be the judge. Give the techniques in here the benefit of the doubt. Try them fully and with an open mind—because if you do, you'll solve a massive pain point in your life.

As one of my students, Joanna, told her friend about working with me, "some of it sounds like it isn't going to work, but try it. It can't hurt! And it worked for me!"

You're going to have the answer to anxious. You're going to *get* to answer to anxious—no longer will you be a passive victim to debilitating anxiety that overwhelms you.

You're going to notice anxiety coming on and then *answer* to it, and it will work.

The *you* on the other side will be the you whom you've always wanted to be—and knew you could be!

Performance anxiety isn't a personal flaw. It's a misguided set of patterns you've fallen into, one that billions of other humans on this planet have fallen into at one point or another in their lives, too.

Now it's time to repattern yourself. You'll go from feeling like a wreck to standing above the crowd as you demonstrate your gifts.

You'll realize that all performance anxiety is the same at its root, and that what works to solve test-taking or social anxiety will work to resolve *any* performance anxiety, be it in public speaking or playing an instrument.

So, let's get into it!

CHAPTER 1

Where Are You on The Spectrum?

"While others panicked, I felt prepared and at ease. This lesson was my secret weapon."

—Chloe, formerly anxious test taker

"This is the first time that I picked up Chelsey from a major test and she seemed happy! It was the first time she said, 'Mom, I finished in time! With ten minutes left on two of the sections, and only three questions I didn't get to on the reading. But normally I have twenty questions I didn't get to!' I LOVE James!"

—Carmen, mother of a formerly anxious test taker

If you have performance anxiety, you deserve *credit*.

You have anxiety because you want to do well!

Performance-anxiety folks—we want it so badly. In fact, we want it too badly, and that's what's messing us up.

After a certain point, trying harder makes things worse.

But if trying hard has gotten us the success we've had so far, how will trying *harder* mess us up?

Let me explain.

In *everything* you do, you are showing up somewhere on a spectrum that's defined by two opposite energies: "play with" energy and "succeed at" energy. This applies as much to an exam as it does to playing a song or video game or having a conversation.

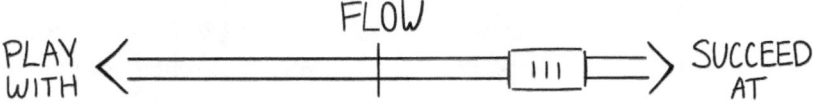

Where you fall on the "play with" versus "succeed at" spectrum will determine *exactly* how it goes. It's a self-fulfilling prophecy.

This spectrum is the landscape of performance anxiety, so let's find out where you've been living on it.

As you come to understand "play with" versus "succeed at," you develop the ability to see where you are on the spectrum at any moment, plus where you need to go in order to perform at your highest level—without anxiety holding you back anymore.

You'll be able to recognize when you're pushing too hard and follow the steps I'll outline to bring you back to the sweet spot in the middle: flow, that state of peak performance.

Let's get to know these two energies.

"Play with" Energy

"Play with" energy is creativity, imagination, and curiosity.

It's play!

It's trying things just to see how they work out, no pressure. It's laughing at mistakes. "Play with" is relaxed and joyful. It's the inner child within each of us. In fact, kids are the best at "play with" energy. They live there all the time.

Too much "play with" energy, though, brings problems: you get sloppy. You lack focus or consistency. You quit when things get hard or serious.

Brazilian soccer players remind me most of "play with" energy. Brazil is famous for "the beautiful game"—soccer played in utter comfort with the ball at one's feet, as if a yo-yo connects the ball to the player's laces.

Brazilians play with dazzling skill, creativity, improvisation, and even a smile (think of Pele, Ronaldo, Ronaldinho, Robinho, Neymar, Marcelo, if you know soccer players).

You might think "play with" will make you less successful, but these guys are among the greatest players to have ever competed.

And yet, Brazilian players can take "play with" too far. As a stereotype, they often become overweight as they get into their late twenties and early thirties. God knows how much eating and partying (*playing!*) a professional soccer player must do to gain weight amidst all the running their sport requires!

Their careers often end early, an inattention to fitness and discipline catching up with them over time.

One could argue that what they needed was more…

"Succeed at" Energy

"Succeed at" energy is the other end of the spectrum. It's determination, resilience, a never-say-die attitude, and working harder! For soccer players, it's showing up to practice every morning at 5am, putting in extra skills work, and watching their diet to a "t" (think Cristiano Ronaldo, soccer fans).

Sounds like the way to succeed, right?

It is, *to an extent*. Too much "succeed at," like too much "play with," backfires as well. That's when you get *too* serious, uptight, and hard on yourself (shifting nervously in your chair as I describe you, dear reader?).

While discipline and hard work will undoubtedly boost your confidence, too much "succeed at" turns into hyper-criticism and excessive work, killing the joy that sustains you and the confidence that unlocks your best performances.

Too much "succeed at" is where performance anxiety emerges.

How can you recognize when *you're* falling too much into "succeed at" energy?

The better you know the geography of "play with" versus "succeed at," not to mention the symptoms of performance anxiety which I'll lay out below, the quicker you'll recognize when you're trying too hard, then readjust back to flow and peak performance.

Over time, you'll gain an intuitive sense for where you are in any moment on the "play with" versus "succeed at" spectrum, and you'll immediately "adjust the dial," so to speak, to bring yourself back to flow.

Keep going: you're going to beat this!

So, allow me to describe your most recent anxiety-ridden performances, when you fell too far into "succeed at"...

(1) Too much "succeed at" starts the moment you decide that mistakes are NOT OK

Have you ever decided this before, that mistakes are not Ok? Have you ever stopped taking risks out of fear, or begun berating yourself over slip-ups?

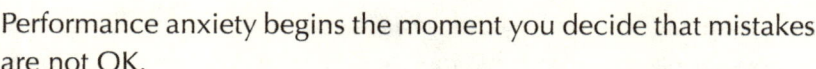

These are signs that you've decided mistakes are not OK.

Performance anxiety begins the moment you decide that mistakes are not OK.

Once you decide mistakes aren't OK,

(2) Perfectionism creeps in

You become petrified that things aren't or won't be perfect.

Right there, you can spot the problem: you're showing up from a feeling of fear, not confidence.

Ever realize that you can *tell* when a tennis player is serving the ball from a place of fear versus a place of confidence?

Or have you felt the difference when someone *says hello* to you from a place of fear versus confidence?

They feel completely different, right? And they produce completely different results.

OK you fearful perfectionist: once fear of mistakes gets ahold of you,

(3) You over-doubt yourself, overthinking what you're doing

Sound like you, yet?

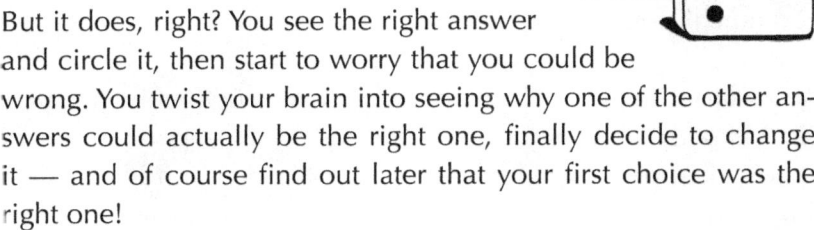

Why is it that overthinking test questions, for example, seems to make us *dumber*?

But it does, right? You see the right answer and circle it, then start to worry that you could be wrong. You twist your brain into seeing why one of the other answers could actually be the right one, finally decide to change it — and of course find out later that your first choice was the right one!

Why did you change it?!

Over-doubting yourself, in anything, is so frustrating.

And now that you're over-doubting and overthinking…

(4) You become rigid and tight

When we overthink, we stop relaxing and flowing. It's as true when you're taking an exam as it was for me trying to have "the perfect conversation" in my social anxiety years (err… decades).

When I was in a conversation and overthinking the interaction, I'd miss little signals like facial expressions or tone of voice from the other person that I'd otherwise have noticed and responded to, if I were more relaxed. As a result, I'd make an ill-timed joke or venture into a topic the other person didn't want to talk about, only later realizing my mistake.

Plunge too far into "succeed at" during a test, and your *focus and attention* over-tighten, too. You know those questions you get wrong where, re-reading it later, you realize how freaking simple the question was, and you can't believe you missed it?

People call them "careless" errors, but they should be called "care-too-much" errors.

You were so much in "succeed at" that your uptight brain could not properly process the text. You missed an important part of the reading passage, or a key word in the question like "NOT" in, "Which of the following answer choices would NOT be acceptable?"

When you tighten up, every part of your being works less well: your singing voice gets constrained, your body dances less in sync with the beat; your throws, kicks, and sprints lose their torque and force.

Notice for yourself right now: when you start stressing, where does your body carry tension?

Too much "succeed at" will *always* make your body tense—this is a law. Each of us carries that tension in a different place: shoulders, neck, stomach, even calves.

For me as I'm writing this, I notice a subtle tension in my temples and chest—remnants of too much "succeed at" energy that I still carry from my past.

Anywhere you're feeling bodily tension is an immediate sign you've dipped too far into "succeed at."

SO, Too Much Succeed At Person! You're terrified of mistakes, over-doubting yourself, overthinking things, and your body and brain are tight now...

This invites the fifth symptom of too much "succeed at"...

(5) You become slower

Tight, over-thinking, full of fear—of course you're moving slowly, now.

How much does this matter when you take a standardized test? I can't tell you how many students I've seen who finish their practice SAT

---

sections relaxedly at home with ten minutes left to spare, then show up for the real test and fail to finish the very same section.

It's like two *completely* different students taking the same test. The same thing can happen for athletes and even social bumblers like I used to be: we become slow and off.

All of this opens the door for our sixth toxic symptom to arrive…

(6) Your self-talk becomes mean, negative, catastrophizing… i.e. CRAZY

How do you talk to yourself when everything we've just described is happening?

Really, really meanly.

Here's an example so you can see how mean this voice gets: questions #47 and #49 on an ACT Math Section seem hard, so you start to freak out. You start to tell yourself, "I'm going to fail this Math Section… I'm going to fail this *test*… I'm not going to get into a good college… My parents are going to be disappointed in me… My friends are going to think I'm stupid… I'm not going to get a good job. I'm not going to make any money in life…"

This sounds *insane*, right?! It was two questions!

Yet so many students I've shared this train of thought with respond with big, knowing grins when I say it out loud to them. It's exactly what they find themselves thinking!

Or maybe you're an actor going in for an audition—the opportunity's amazing and the part fits you so well! But the second you

---

ANSWER TO ANXIOUS

forget a word, you start to think you've blown it. You'll never get this part now. You're never going to get *any* roles, in fact. You're going to have to quit acting and work in something else that you hate. Then life will suck...

We catastrophize.

If you've ever thought this way, you're not alone. You're in the *majority*. No shame in it. We all get this silly sometimes.

Here's the thing: this negative self-talk is extremely inaccurate. It's so far from what's true.

Try to remember times you spoke to yourself this meanly — looking back, was that voice really balanced or accurate?

No!

But in those stressed moments, we tend to believe the crazy talk. And no one can perform at their best when they're listening to insult after insult, distortion after distortion, in their own minds.

Amidst this mental environment...

(7) Your confidence PLUMMETS

How important is confidence for performing at your best?

Extremely!

No wonder you've been doing so poorly each time you showed up in too much "succeed at" energy.

After a certain point, by trying harder, you can make yourself *worse*.

"Play with" versus "succeed at": it all makes sense now, right?

Once you get a feeling for the spectrum, you'll start to catch yourself when you slip too far in one direction or the other, just like pilots flying east from San Francisco to New York who notice themselves moving off-course if they veer too far north or south during the flight.

When that happens, they readjust their direction, back to center. And that's exactly what you'll learn to do, in every part of your life, as you absorb this book.

Feel yourself getting tight or talking meanly to yourself? Loosen your grip, relax your body, speak kinder to yourself. Come back to center. You'll perform better there.

Before we move on, re-read the table below, summarizing what happens when we go too far into "succeed at." Memorize those points, because the better you know them, and the quicker they come to mind, the faster you'll catch yourself when you've dipped too far into "succeed at."

The 7 Symptoms of Too Much Succeed At

1. Mistakes NOT Ok
2. Perfectionist
3. Over-doubting
4. Rigid & Tight
5. Moving Slower
6. Catastrophizing
7. Confidence PLUMMETS

In the next chapter, you'll figure out how to escape that pit of quicksand!

Joe's Story: When Too Much "Succeed At" Nearly Killed Business School Success

Joe came to me while preparing for his GMAT. Working at a prestigious investment bank in New York City, he had high aspirations for business school: only Harvard, Wharton, Stanford, or Columbia would do, in his mind.

His problem was that his practice GMATs were scoring in the 500s, and he needed at least a 700 to have a chance at one of these schools. He was miles from where he needed to be.

Joe had already completed two GMAT prep classes, but no matter how hard he tried, he couldn't get his scores out of the 500s.

And trying too hard was exactly his problem.

After I explained to him the "play with" versus "succeed at" spectrum, his eureka moment arrived. He realized he'd been "playing defense" on his GMATs, as he put it, and he needed to be "playing offense" instead. He had become petrified to make mistakes, which caused him to spend too long on questions.

He needed to get rid of his fear of mistakes, pronto.

Joe started to play with trusting that his best effort was good enough as he solved a problem. If he was eighty percent sure of his answer, he decided to go with it, instead of doubting himself and spending even longer on the question.

Maybe he'd get it wrong, but that was OK. He had to move on and answer more questions in order to score more points.

The breakthroughs started to come: a 620 on a practice test, then a 670.

In the end, Joe scored a 720 on his real GMAT, good enough to help him gain acceptance to Columbia Business School. For someone so committed to succeeding, learning to relax his "succeed at" energy proved to be Joe's winning breakthrough.

KEY POINTS

CHAPTER 1: WHERE ARE YOU ON THE SPECTRUM?

Too much "succeed at" starts the moment...

1. You decide that mistakes are NOT OK

2. Perfectionist fear creeps in

3. You over-doubt yourself, overthinking what you're doing

4. You become rigid and tight—even in your thinking

5. You become slower

6. Your self-talk becomes mean, negative, and catastrophizing

7. Your confidence PLUMMETS

Remember: tension in the body is a sign of too much "succeed at," and nearly everything the mean, negative, and catastrophizing self-talk says to you amidst too much "succeed at" is *not* true!

JOURNAL / REFLECT

CHAPTER 1: WHERE ARE YOU ON THE SPECTRUM?

1. Where in your life have you decided, or acted like, mistakes are not OK? How much better could you have performed in this part of life if you had *accepted* that mistakes were OK?

2. Notice in which parts of life might you be a perfectionist. Could it be with your style, or your athletics, or your test scores or grades?

3. What are two CRAZY things your negative self-talk has told you in the past when you were feeling stressed? Stop and find two specific things your mind has told you.

CHAPTER 2

Back into Balance

"After just one session [on "play with" versus "succeed at"], I saw a change in Alex. The weight of anxiety lifted, replaced by a newfound confidence."

—Erin, parent of a formerly anxious musician

"I needed a 34 on the ACT in order to get a major scholarship in Oklahoma, where I grew up. I ended up taking the ACT *nine* times trying to get it. At one point, I scored five straight 29s. I wasn't even close to the score I needed. But I knew it was anxiety that was messing me up. It wasn't until my last try, at the end of senior year when I'd stopped caring finally, that all of a sudden, I scored a 34 and got the scholarship I needed."

—Sam, formerly anxious test taker

So where have *you* been dipping too much into "succeed at"?

When I was in middle school, I was obsessed with basketball, and I took 200-300 jump shots every day, no matter what, even in rain or snow. Gradually, I developed the best jump shot in my grade. My "succeed at" work ethic had its benefits!

I made the town all-star team, a huge accomplishment for me, but when I got into the games, I felt petrified of shooting. I was afraid I'd anger my teammates by missing. Because I didn't shoot, I didn't score, and soon enough, my coach realized I wasn't very valuable to have on the court. I barely played.

I made the same mistake socially: I was horrified of saying or doing something that someone might judge or make fun of, so I became incredibly uptight in conversation.

Consider taking my Social Skills for Life class. I'm so passionate about the skills and ideas in that class that I gave up SAT tutoring to focus entirely on teaching them. (www.growthwise.us/social-skills) And as a thank you for reading this book, use the code answertoanxious at checkout for $20 off "Make Them Feel Seen" or answertoanxious2 for $100 off "Social Skills for Life."]

Wherever you find yourself going too far into "succeed at," let's fix this habit—*for life.*

Come backwards along the "play with" versus "succeed at" spectrum towards a healthy balance between the two.

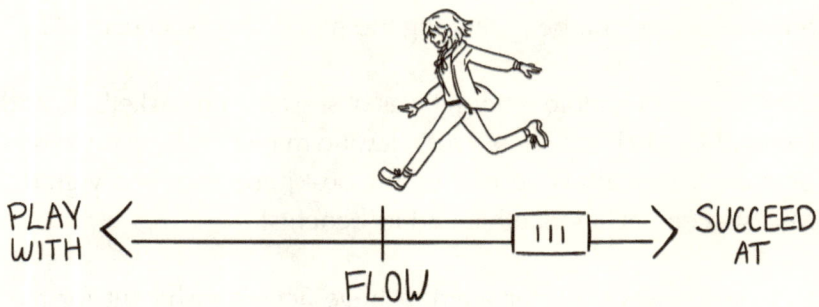

PLAY WITH $\longleftrightarrow$ SUCCEED AT

FLOW

Imagine you're in *balance* between "play with" and "succeed at": you've got the joy, inspiration, fun, and creativity of "play with" *and* the discipline, consistency, focus, and work ethic of healthy "succeed at."

That sweet spot in the middle is what I call "flow."

"Play with" is the joy, the creativity, the spontaneity—the energy or river of life, in a way.

"Succeed at" is the structured banks of the river—making sure that river of energy flows *somewhere* and doesn't just spill out over the ground aimlessly.

Too much "play with" and you're scattered, aimless. Too much "succeed at" and you're directed but cutting off the flow, *missing* the juice, joy, confidence, and enthusiasm.

Balance between the two and now you've got life force *and* direction.

Guess how I would've played basketball as a kid if I'd known how to find flow?

I'd have practiced every day after school just like I did, but in the games, I'd let my shot fly. We call it "playing" basketball, for a reason. Sports at their best, like music, are still *play*.

I actually think I could've been one of the top scorers, if not *the* top scorer, on my teams, if I'd known how to stay at the "flow" point between "play with" and "succeed at."

But what was I instead, mired in too much "succeed at" energy?

A bench-warmer, who left games in a sulk, cried in his room at home, and then resolved to practice even harder going forward, as if that would fix everything. But "practice more" had already been my go-to "more succeed at" answer, and obviously it wasn't working. I'd show up to the next game just as scared to make a mistake.

Sound familiar, you 1500-scoring practice SAT-takers in your bedroom who show up to the actual SAT and somehow produce a 1320 instead?

The journey back to a healthy balance with "play with" begins with the following six bullet points, each one logically following the previous one.

Remember how performance anxiety begins with your having decided that mistakes are not OK?

In flow, the healthy balance between "play with" and "succeed at"...

(1) You decide to perceive mistakes as OK!

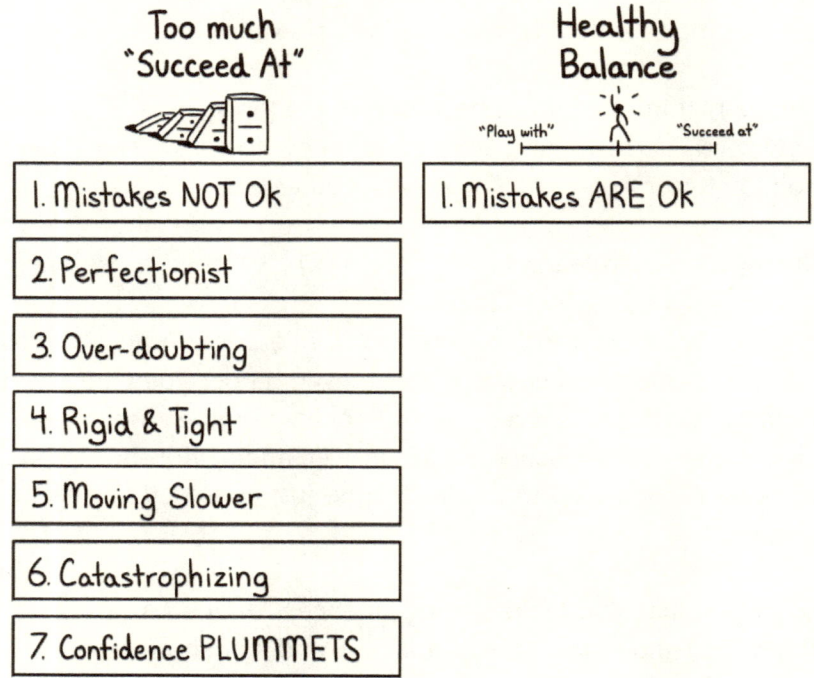

Too much "Succeed At"	Healthy Balance
1. Mistakes NOT Ok	1. Mistakes ARE Ok
2. Perfectionist	
3. Over-doubting	
4. Rigid & Tight	
5. Moving Slower	
6. Catastrophizing	
7. Confidence PLUMMETS	

Everyone makes mistakes, constantly, including the people you think are perfect.

Think of an actor, singer, or athlete whom you're convinced is perfect at what they do. Watch them after their *best* performance, and if you asked them afterwards how they did, they'd probably be able to tell you twenty different mistakes they made.

Ben Hogan was the best golfer in the world in the 1940s and '50s. In his best golf rounds, he shot around a sixty-five. Guess how many shots he said were "perfect" in those rounds?

Four.

The other sixty-one shots, by the best golfer in the world, during his very best rounds, were mistakes. Things he could have done better!

Are you breathing? Are you human?

Then you are a veritable mistake-making machine. And you always will be.

There is no escaping mistakes, so let's stop fearing them.

Your *relationship* to mistakes, rather than you making them or not, is what needs to change.

I used to be so afraid of mistakes that I would try to figure everything out in my head first, so that when I finally did take action, I would be perfect! Unassailable!

If only that worked. I'd think about the girl I had a crush on and wonder what to say to her and how and when and what if I did it this way, but then what if I did it that way. (Spot the overthinking?)

Then guess what would happen?

Nothing. I wouldn't say anything! And then I'd jump back into ruminating about the next time she came near, so that maybe *this* time I'd finally know the right thing to say to her.

All of this was incredibly attractive to these girls, as I'm sure you can tell.

You know how you get better at talking to someone you like? *By talking to them.* By *trying it out*, and finding out from experience what works and what doesn't.

Mistakes tend to be the BEST ways to learn.

Tom Brady is believed by many to be the greatest NFL quarterback of all time. He often says, "there is no losing—only winning and learning" (I've heard three-time Olympic gold medalist snowboarder Shaun White say the exact same thing).

Brady would know! At the University of Michigan, he began his career as the seventh-string quarterback. When he attempted his very first pass in a college game, he threw an interception that was returned by the other team for a touchdown.

Twenty years later, he is the winningest professional quarterback to ever play the game.

To escape too much "succeed at," **decide to adopt a new belief about mistakes. Embrace them** as constant, normal, and *vital* to learning and success. They are your best teachers!

Repeat after me: *mistakes are my path to success*! Mistakes are my path to success!

So that's #1: Decide to experience mistakes differently, and your fear of them will fade.

Ready to do that? Great! I'll also recommend that you print the following drawing by my wonderful illustrator Angela Chiang, and put it in a few different places like your bathroom mirror or next to the door of your bedroom so you see it each time you exit.

What do you notice about this path to success?

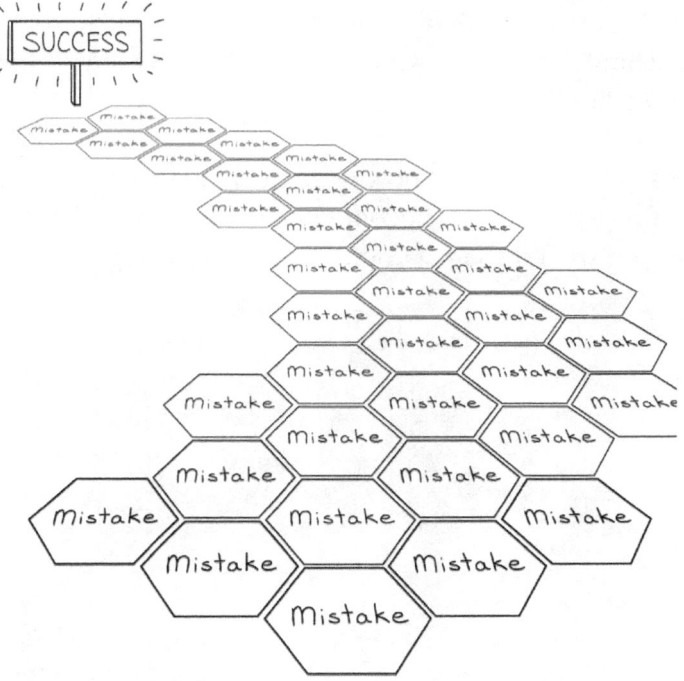

The more mistakes you make, the further along you get.

When I was 28, I did a series of drawings. I hadn't drawn since high school, which was the height of my neurotic perfectionism, and these drawings twelve years later became meditations on giving up perfectionism.

If I sensed that my hand didn't want to draw anymore, I would put down the pen I was drawing with and stop for the day. Old me would have pushed forward, needing the image to be "perfect," and kept drawing!

But that too much "succeed at" version of me had robbed all the joy from drawing, such that I hadn't wanted to do it in twelve years.

When I shared my 28-year-old self's drawings with a friend from high school, he was blown away: "Dude! You weren't this good in high school!"

I guess not! Just went to show how much better and more expressive of a performer we become when we dare to dial back our perfectionism. I'll share a couple of these drawings:

A life that could have been - scene from "American Beauty." Pen and ink.

Rest on a New York City subway. Pen and ink.

Have you shifted your perspective on mistakes yet?

Amazing. Now, in this healthy balance between "play with" and "succeed at," you …

(2&3) Trust that your best is good enough

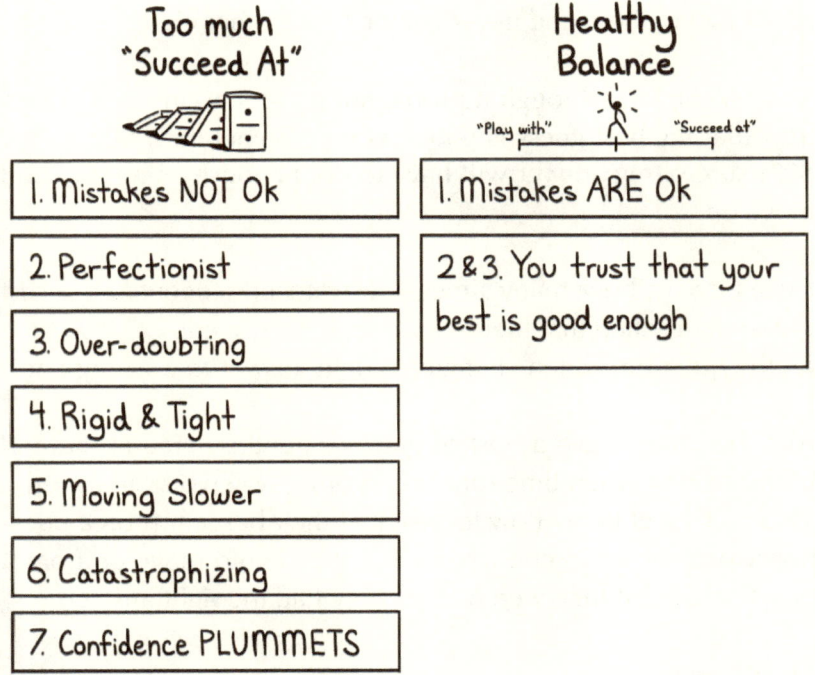

Too much "Succeed At"	Healthy Balance
1. Mistakes NOT Ok	1. Mistakes ARE Ok
2. Perfectionist	2 & 3. You trust that your best is good enough
3. Over-doubting	
4. Rigid & Tight	
5. Moving Slower	
6. Catastrophizing	
7. Confidence PLUMMETS	

How exhausting was it to over-doubt yourself and overthink everything?

Try something different, now: decide to trust that your best is good enough.

With a Harvard degree and two decades' SAT and ACT tutoring experience, I am probably expected by my students to breeze through standardized tests when I take them. Believe me: on more questions than they'd ever guess, I'm not quite sure what the right answer is.

But I know I don't have forever to think about the question. I have to move on to get to the other questions. Half-way thinking my way through ten questions will score higher than fully thinking about two of them and never getting to the other eight.

So after thinking through a problem a good amount, I decide to trust that my best guess is good enough. Sometimes, being only 80% sure of my answer will have to do; I choose an answer and move on.

I can't count how many times I've watched students on a test question, terrified that their answer is wrong, spend *way* too long on the question—often changing a right answer to a wrong one!

And then they leave a host of questions unanswered at the end of the section when time runs out, scoring *way* worse in the end. They didn't yet know how to trust that their best effort on a question would be good enough, so that they could move on from a question even if they weren't *sure* they had the right answer.

Make sense?

Now, remember how rigid and tight we became in last chapters' description of too much "succeed at"?

In the healthy balance between the two energies, instead of becoming rigid and tight...

(4) You're relaxed and responsive

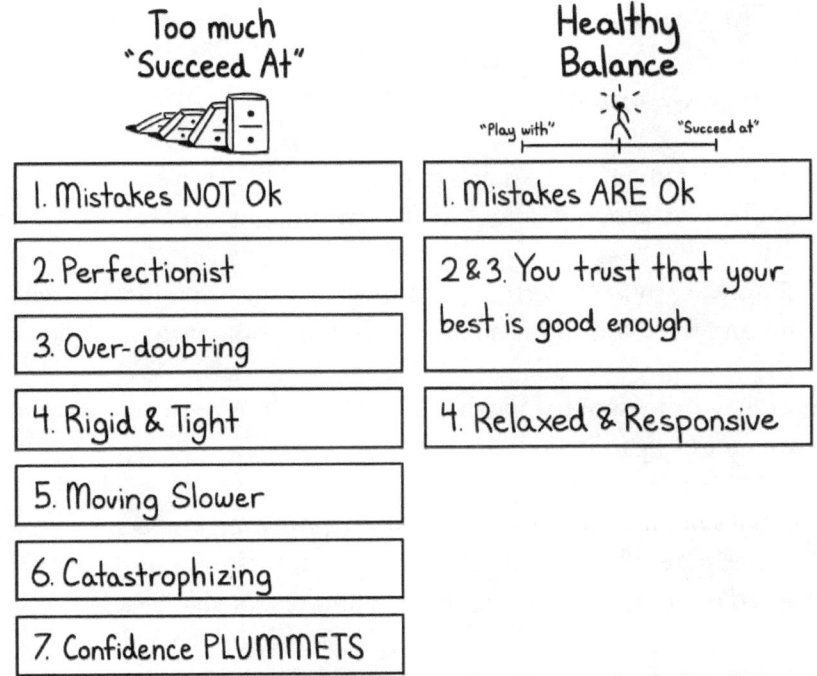

Too much "Succeed At"	Healthy Balance
1. Mistakes NOT Ok	1. Mistakes ARE Ok
2. Perfectionist	2&3. You trust that your best is good enough
3. Over-doubting	
4. Rigid & Tight	4. Relaxed & Responsive
5. Moving Slower	
6. Catastrophizing	
7. Confidence PLUMMETS	

When you're relaxed and responsive, *you absorb the reading passage or test question as you read it.* You read the defense correctly in the game, and you naturally respond to the social cues in the conversation.

When you're relaxed and responsive, you stop missing key details.

I'll never forget walking through the halls of my high school one day during senior year with my classmate EK. EK always seemed relaxed and charming, comfortable with himself in a way that I admired.

As we walked, my mind started to race with fears about what I should say to him. As I became more uptight, a pregnant silence grew between us,

"Awwwwk-waaaarrrd!" he finally blurted out.

I was crushed. EK didn't say it to be mean. He was just expressing what he was experiencing: I really was being awkward!

I simply wasn't relaxed and responsive in my interaction with him, and that caused my social IQ in that moment to plummet.

Ever have the same thing happen to you during a test or performance?

Well, it's *not* the kind of thing that happens when you accept mistakes as a healthy part of any experience, trusting that your best is good enough, and feeling relaxed and responsive as a result.

Meanwhile, in that healthy balance between "play with" and "succeed at"...

(5) You move gracefully and quickly

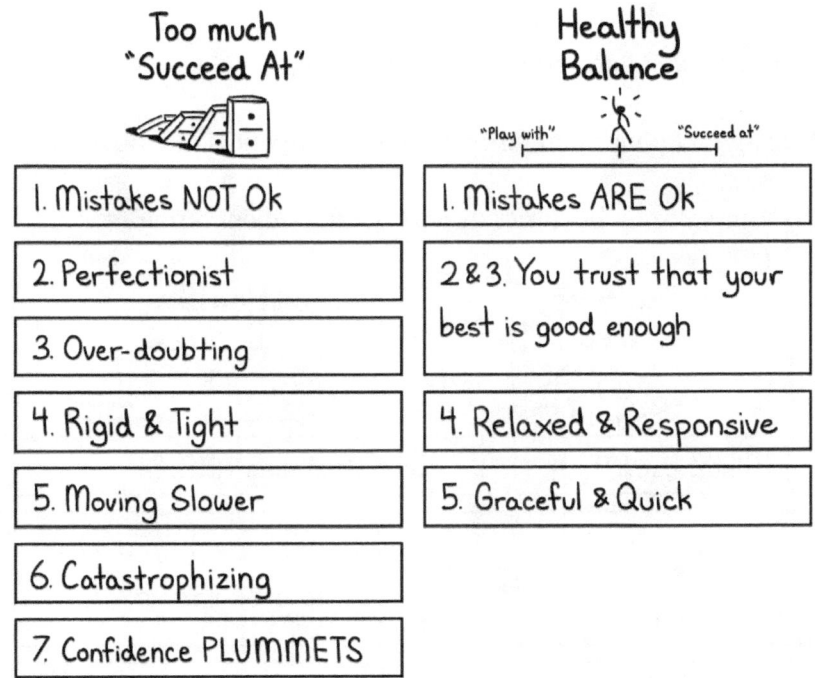

Too much "Succeed At"	Healthy Balance
1. Mistakes NOT Ok	1. Mistakes ARE Ok
2. Perfectionist	2 & 3. You trust that your best is good enough
3. Over-doubting	
4. Rigid & Tight	4. Relaxed & Responsive
5. Moving Slower	5. Graceful & Quick
6. Catastrophizing	
7. Confidence PLUMMETS	

Jokes roll off your tongue in conversation. You pull up and shoot the basketball in the short time you're open (instead of holding the ball and letting the defense collapse on you, like my middle-school self would do).

You raise your hand instantly when the theater director asks who'd like to play a certain part — and because you didn't hesitate, suddenly the part is yours.

Of course you move through exam questions quicker. It all makes sense, right?

So you accept now that mistakes will happen. You trust that your best is good enough.

You're relaxed and responsive, and moving quicker, too!

Guess what your inner emotional environment is like now?

(6) Your self-talk becomes honest, kind, and encouraging

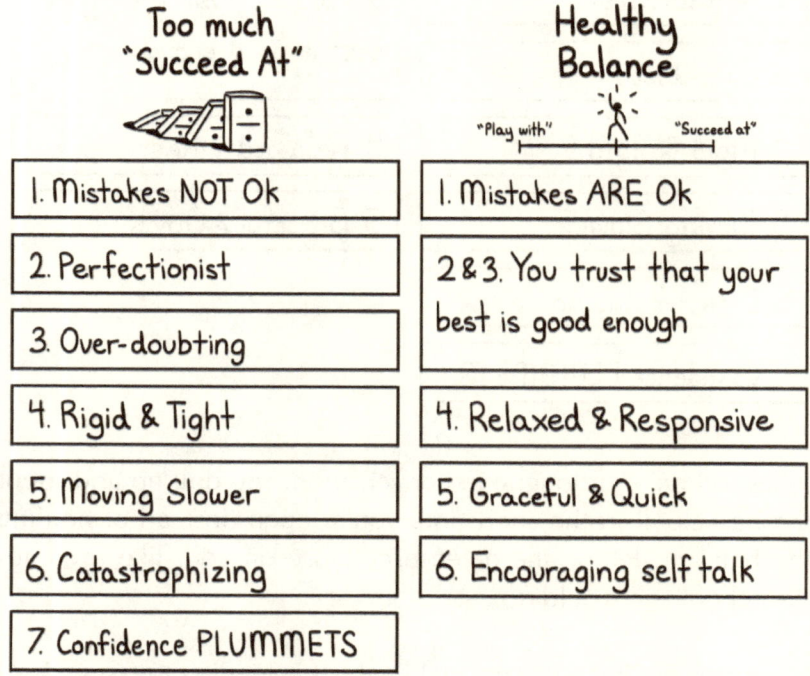

Too much "Succeed At"	Healthy Balance
1. Mistakes NOT Ok	1. Mistakes ARE Ok
2. Perfectionist	2 & 3. You trust that your best is good enough
3. Over-doubting	
4. Rigid & Tight	4. Relaxed & Responsive
5. Moving Slower	5. Graceful & Quick
6. Catastrophizing	6. Encouraging self talk
7. Confidence PLUMMETS	

Remember the scenario last chapter where questions #47 and #49 in the ACT Math Section were hard? Instead of writing off your future as a failure in that next moment, when you're in flow, you find yourself thinking something like, "Wow. Those were hard. Maybe I got them right, maybe not. Let me see what I can do on the next questions. Maybe I'll still score well."

Your self-talk becomes honest, kind, and encouraging.

That's how we speak to ourselves when we're in a healthy balance of "play with" and "succeed at".

Grounded, optimistic, but honest self-talk doesn't make questions #47 and #49 into anything more than two hard questions on a math section.

This self-talk is WAY more accurate and truthful. Could you have gotten those two math questions wrong? Sure! You acknowledge that. But you're also honest in the positive direction: you might've gotten them right, and you might score well even if you *did* get them wrong.

Finally, we return to the most important factor of all: *confidence*.

In a healthy balance, where you accept mistakes, trust your best is good enough, feel relaxed and responsive, move quicker, and talk to yourself in kind, honest, and encouraging words...

(7) Your confidence RISES

Too much "Succeed At"	Healthy Balance
1. Mistakes NOT Ok	1. Mistakes ARE Ok
2. Perfectionist	2 & 3. You trust that your best is good enough
3. Over-doubting	
4. Rigid & Tight	4. Relaxed & Responsive
5. Moving Slower	5. Graceful & Quick
6. Catastrophizing	6. Encouraging self talk
7. Confidence PLUMMETS	7. Confidence RISES

How important is confidence to you performing at your best?

Do we even need to answer that?!

As much as you used to believe that the answer to more success was to press harder into "succeed at," I hope you're waking up to the truth, now.

Too much "succeed at" *kills success.*

After a certain point, more is less.

It's like deciding that because pasta needs to be cooked in boiling water, the longer you cook it in boiling water, the better it will taste!

Nope! You'd turn it into mush.

Performing at your best, like cooking pasta, is a delicate balance, a sweet spot in the middle, where all the magic happens.

That Magical Balance: A Sweet Spot Called "Flow"

Have you ever been "in flow" before?

Time seemed to slow down. You were *so* present in the moment, as you sang, played the part, drained game-winning foul shots, or reveled in jokes with friends.

Paradoxically, time passed so quickly at the same time.

All your gifts came out. Your voice hit those notes so purely!

The foul shots splashed softly straight through the net, like you knew they would.

This is what happens when you find the balance between "play with" and "succeed at." You enter that flow state.

And in flow, *all* of your intelligence comes out, effortlessly: social intelligence, emotional intelligence, test-taking intelligence, etc.!

In flow, you *surprise* yourself with how good what just came out of you really was.

How would you like to experience that every day? In the coming chapters, you'll learn to access flow and stay there for good.

Sam's Story: A Flutist Finds Flow

Sam came to me as a sophomore in high school. An expert competitive flutist with an upcoming audition for Cincinnati's elite high school orchestra, Sam had developed a habit of making mistakes during major auditions.

Sam wanted help, but he was *convinced* that my first principle of moving out of too much "succeed at" was simply not true in his case: for him to be accepted into the high-level ensembles, summer programs, or universities that he aspired to, he had to be perfect. A mistake would get him rejected, he was sure.

You can imagine the perfectionist fear that belief infected his playing with!

The key for me was to show Sam how destructive that fear of mistakes was to his ability to play beautiful music. He couldn't perform with grace, timing, and emotion if his body became tight and rigid as he played.

After seeing the value in aspiring towards the sweet spot between "play with" and "succeed at," Sam crushed it in the recitals and auditions that followed.

His mom sent an email about our session with the subject line "Money well-spent":

> "I wanted to tell you how valuable Sam found your session on Friday night. He did AMAZINGLY well at his

recital yesterday, and was really working to put into practice some of the new thinking models you gave him."

A few weeks later, Sam wrote me that he'd been accepted into the Cincinnati Symphony Youth Orchestra:

"I have learned to focus all of my energy into joy instead of wasting my energy on a few little things that could go wrong. I messed up terribly in one part of the audition, but all of my other stuff was pretty much how I wanted it to be, and I still got in. Now I can truly believe, rather than just trying to convince myself, that mistakes ACTUALLY ARE ok, because I still got in. I need to be more confident that I truly prepared well for it, and even with some mistakes, my preparation will pay off. With that in mind, I'm sure my auditions in the future will be even better as long as I play for fun, and accept that mistakes will happen. I'm finally grasping the idea of "play with" energy, I still had some nerves, but only a small amount that did not affect my performance!"

KEY POINTS

CHAPTER 2: BACK INTO BALANCE

To come back to flow, the sweet spot between "play with" and "succeed at"...

1. You decide to see mistakes as OK

2. You trust that your best is good enough

3. You become relaxed and responsive

4. You move gracefully and quickly

5. Your self-talk becomes honest, kind, and encouraging

6. Your confidence RISES

JOURNAL / REFLECT

CHAPTER 2: BACK INTO BALANCE

1. Where in your life do you *accept* your mistakes? Might you be approaching that part of your life in flow?

2. What's something where you notice you're relaxed when you do it, while others often aren't so relaxed as you? Do you tend to perform better than they do?

3. Who are some of your favorite performers (athletes, performers, comedians even) who clearly perform from a place of flow, grace, and fluidity? What can you imagine they do to make sure they don't slip too far into "succeed at"—despite the huge pressure under which they perform?

CHAPTER 3

Know Your Nervous System

"The parasympathetic skill has been aiding me a lot! I was scaring myself into second thoughts on dropping from a student government race because I was intimidated by my competition. I have been using the breathing every time that fear crawled back and it has been helping me!"

—Angel, formerly anxious social skills student

"I am truly shocked to see just how much of a confidence booster this class has been... I've grown. I learned to love myself more, and I learned how to put things into perspective. Coming from somebody who has always struggled with anxiety, this tool is something that has been extremely beneficial to me."

—Shannon, formerly anxious social skills student

Knowing what it looks and feels like to return to flow, as the last chapter showed you, is key. But my experience helping hundreds of people resolve performance anxiety has shown me that to become expert at *staying* in flow, you need a deeper understanding of the nervous system. Let's give you that now.

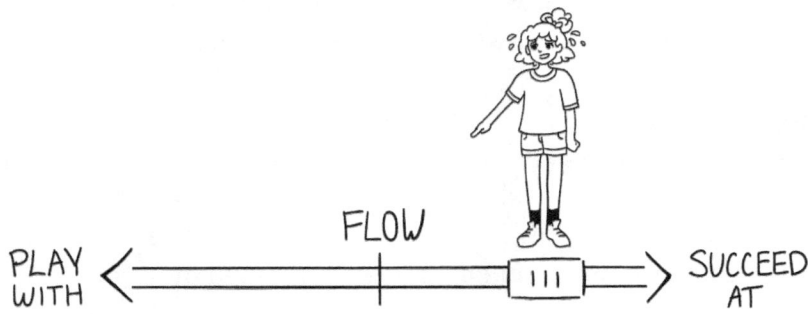

Your nervous system is made up of your brain, spinal cord, and nerves. It regulates just about every major system of your body: heart beat, breathing, immune system, moods, hormones, etc. It's the master system!

At any moment, your nervous system is moving in either of two directions: towards a _sympathetic_ nervous system response or a _parasympathetic_ nervous system response. Don't worry: I'll give you easy ways to remember these science-y sounding names.

Let's break down your sympathetic nervous system response, first—this is the one you're too deep in when you're having performance anxiety.

Your Sympathetic Nervous System Response

Your sympathetic response is designed to activate you in response to survival threats. Think of it as your stress or "sweat" response (way to remember: "S-S-S," sympathetic, stress, sweat).

In sympathetic, your heart beats quicker, your breath becomes more shallow, and your body starts pumping stress hormones like cortisol into your blood. Sounds like performance anxiety!

Too much of this over the long term and your body begins to break down: excess cortisol production leads to the loss of bone density, memory, skin elasticity (read: you look older), and immune system function. You even begin to accumulate a certain type of unhealthy fat around your belly from too much cortisol.

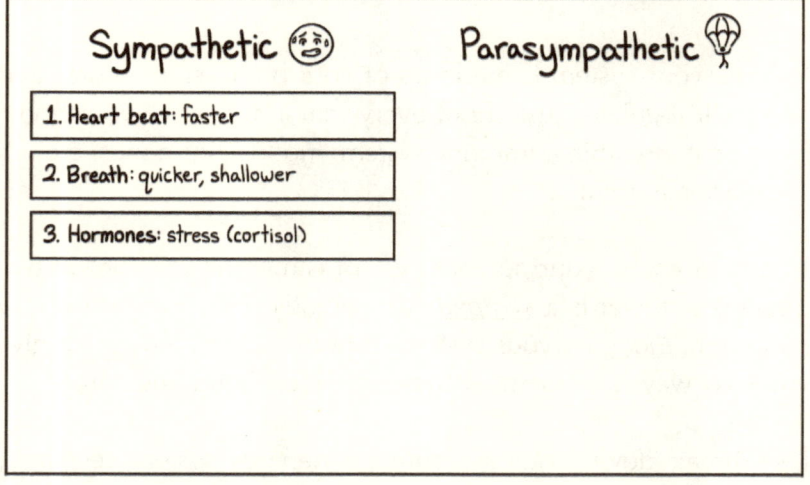

Here's a crazy fact: almost every mammal on earth experiences the same number of heartbeats across an average lifetime: one billion. A mouse that lives two years will experience a billion heartbeats (albeit at a much faster rate), just like a human or elephant who lives 80 years will live through a billion heartbeats (at a much slower rate).

So: how fast is your heart might be beating right now? Can you see that as you learn to calm your nervous system, and slow your own heartbeat down, you're adding time to your life?

As your breath, heart rate, and hormones shift, your emotions will, too. As you slip too far into sympathetic, you'll start to feel alone in the world. You could be *surrounded* by friends and loved ones, but if you're in a stressed and anxious state, you'll still feel alone in the world.

Finally, and for many students this is the most important symptom to look out for: in sympathetic, the voice in your head becomes critical, fearful, and mean!

This is worth repeating five times to yourself just to get it into your mind: in sympathetic, the voice in your head becomes critical, fearful, and mean. Critical, fearful, and mean!

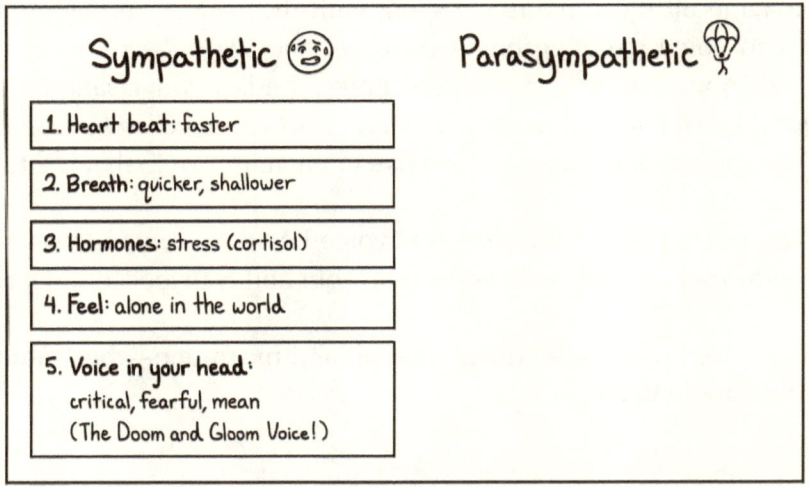

Does this sound like the voice that speaks when you're stuck in performance anxiety?

You bet it does!

Are you realizing how much WORSE you become—at everything!—in a sympathetic nervous system state, when you're stuck in too much "succeed at"?

Now will you please take the lessons of this book and stop doing that?

Don't be like me and require three decades before you finally figure all this out for yourself.

Remember those times in your past, before you understood your nervous system, when you'd spin out into stress, and you'd stay in that state for a *long* time? Like hours, days, weeks, or even years?

I did that, too.

Imagine all those hours we spent with the critical, fearful, and mean voice narrating our lives to us, and we *believed* what it said! About our grades and test scores, the last conversation we just had (*You idiot! You shouldn't have said X! You could have said Y!*), and about what we looked like in the mirror or in that photo.

Can you see what believing that voice has done to your self-esteem? Your capacity to love yourself? Your ability to feel confident?

I call this voice—the critical, fearful, and mean one—**the Doom and Gloom Voice**.

Here's my belief: 99% of what the Doom and Gloom Voice says is NOT true.

Stop believing it so much!

Starting now, when you hear the Doom and Gloom Voice start to speak, you'll have a totally different response: you'll notice the 99%-factually-inaccurate voice speaking, and disregard it!

You'll take it purely as a signal that it's time to move your nervous system back into a parasympathetic state. *That* is your answer to anxious.

Your Parasympathetic Nervous System Response

Your "parasympathetic self" is 1,000x better at life: it rolls through pressure while staying in flow! So let's get to know it now.

In parasympathetic, your heart beat slows down (and we saw what that does to life span).

Your breath slows down, deepens, and becomes lighter, too.

Instead of pumping stress hormones, your parasympathetic response pumps a wellbeing hormone known as DHEA. Known as the "vitality hormone" for its anti-aging properties, DHEA repairs tissue and boosts your mood and immune system.

Remember how in sympathetic you start to feel alone in the world? In parasympathetic, you instinctively see others as "you *and* me."

Sympathetic 😖	Parasympathetic 🪂
1. Heart beat: faster	1. Heart beat: slower
2. Breath: quicker, shallower	2. Breath: slower, deeper, lighter
3. Hormones: stress (cortisol)	3. Hormones: vitality & wellbeing (DHEA)
4. Feel: alone in the world	
5. Voice in your head: critical, fearful, mean (The Doom and Gloom Voice!)	

You know those moments where you're feeling relaxed and generous or loving towards others? Those moments of connection take place when your nervous system is in a more parasympathetic state.

You can be hiking or meditating in the woods, all alone, but in a deeply parasympathetic state, you'll feel connected to everything around you.

Finally, the voice in your head is very different in parasympathetic: it's honest, compassionate, and wise. I call this voice **Inner Wisdom**.

We *all* have access to Inner Wisdom within us—a voice that knows the truth, has common sense, handles life gracefully, and can smell BS from a mile away. You can tap into your Inner Wisdom at any time, *but you cannot hear your Inner Wisdom until you get yourself into a parasympathetic state first.*

Let me show you a scenario so you can start to hear the difference between your sympathetic Doom and Gloom Voice and your parasympathetic Inner Wisdom.

Imagine you're preparing for an exam and you get a disappointing score. What does your sympathetic nervous system probably say?

> *You idiot. You screwed it up. All that studying was a waste of time. You're never going to get where you want to go. People are going to think you're stupid. You're never going to get a good job or make any money... That girl or guy you like? You're not getting them either.*

On and on it goes! It might say even more!

Now, what does your parasympathetic voice say after the disappointing test score?

> *That's frustrating. I put a lot of time into studying for this test, and I still don't have close to the score I want. There must be things I'm still doing wrong and need to change. I'll relax today. But tomorrow, I'll make a list of the areas on the test I'm still weak in and come up with a plan for how I can get better. I won't quit—I'll just keep learning what I need to until I get where I need to go.*

Notice the Inner Wisdom voice doesn't just shower you in praise: *Oh, you're the smartest, the best. You'll surely ace the test next time!*

It's compassionate, but it's also honest and wise: *you're weak in these areas, so here's the positive step we're going to take next to address that.*

Sympathetic 😵	Parasympathetic 🪂
1. Heart beat: faster	1. Heart beat: slower
2. Breath: quicker, shallower	2. Breath: slower, deeper, lighter
3. Hormones: stress (cortisol)	3. Hormones: vitality & wellbeing (DHEA)
4. Feel: alone in the world	4. Feel: connected to others
5. Voice in your head: critical, fearful, mean (The Doom and Gloom Voice!)	5. Voice in your head: honest, compassionate, wise (Inner Wisdom)

Think of "parasympathetic" as your "parachute response." When a parachute catches your fall during skydiving, you go from falling precipitously to suddenly gliding calmly and easily through the sky. Meanwhile, from all the way up there, you're gifted a "zoomed out" view of the entire landscape. Everything looks small, and the whole scene is beautiful.

In a parasympathetic state, you can see events for how small they are in the grand scheme of things, and life looks a lot more beautiful.

By contrast, notice how BIG everything looks when you're stressed, in sympathetic? How disproportionately large you perceive problems that you later realize were small?

Stay in parasympathetic. See life for what it really is, as the Inner Wisdom voice shows you in its honest, wise, and compassionate voice. Learn to relax and trust that you're good, you're safe, and things aren't nearly as catastrophic as the Doom and Gloom voice would try to make you believe.

Armed with this nervous system knowledge, you're ready to move out of sympathetic and too much "succeed at," back to parasympathetic and flow.

Mila's Story: Long California State Tests Scare Her No More

Mila was a seventh grader who found herself blanking out on the long California state tests she and her classmates had to take.

"I'm always stressed on tests," she said. "I feel very anxious and have a hard time focusing. My mind will be wandering. I'll be thinking about nothing and everything all at the same time."

On a three-day state test during the Spring, her first two days were anxious and dismal, but on the third day she finally tried the light-and-slow nose breath to move herself into parasympathetic as she took the exam (a technique described in the next chapter).

"I felt more centered," she said. "My mind definitely wandered less. Every once in a while it still did, but it was way easier to keep focused. I could feel myself really thinking through the questions, and into them, not just shallow thinking like I'd do before."

After that success, she made sure to move herself into parasympathetic on a major math test for school. On the previous three math tests, she'd scored in the 85th percentile. But on this one, she scored in the 96th percentile!

"I felt awesome, getting my score back," she said. "I'm way more confident just seeing how well I can do now."

KEY POINTS

CHAPTER 3: KNOW YOUR NERVOUS SYSTEM

In a sympathetic nervous system response...

- Your heart beats faster

- Your breath quickens and becomes shallow

- Your body produces stress hormones

- You feel more alone in the world

- The voice in your head becomes critical, fearful, and mean!

In a parasympathetic nervous system response...

- Your heart beats slower

- Your breath slows and deepens

- Your body produces wellbeing hormones

- You feel connected to others

- The voice in your head is honest, compassionate, and wise!

Ninety-nine percent of what's said by the Doom and Gloom Voice of your sympathetic nervous system is NOT true!

We *all* have a voice of Inner Wisdom inside of us, but we cannot access it unless we move ourselves into a parasympathetic state (the topic of the next chapter!).

JOURNAL / REFLECT

CHAPTER 3: KNOW YOUR NERVOUS SYSTEM

1. What are some of the most common Doom and Gloom Voice things your sympathetic nervous system says to you? Does it tell you you're unattractive, or an idiot, or never going to succeed at something?

2. What's a moment where you noticed someone else's Doom and Gloom Voice talking them into a way-too-negative perception of a situation? How did that person's believing the Doom and Gloom Voice affect how the situation played out?

3. When was the last time you felt like you were in a parasympathetic state? What did that feel like?

Find Flow in Parasympathetic

"With the mental health issues going on in the world, my daughter had three or four panic attacks in 2020. Hannah really gravitated toward the mind-body work that you were doing, and she hasn't had a panic attack since working with you."

—Kat, mother of a formerly anxious student

"I feel like I have a way now, from the class, that I can be more relaxed all the time, which is very nice. The thing I use the most is breathing and activating my parasympathetic mode. Now it's easy to tell which nervous system mode I'm in. I used to be in sympathetic all the time, while pretending I was relaxed, but I wasn't. It's easy to put myself into a better place now."

—Brendan, formerly socially anxious student

This chapter gives you three go-to moves that you'll do in the heat of the moment, as you feel yourself slipping into sympathetic and stress, that will bring you back to parasympathetic and flow. *These are your answers to anxious.*

"FLOW MOVE" 1: *Breathe as Slowly and Lightly Through Your Nose as You Can*

This one sounds too simple—*annoyingly* too simple. But it *works*. You just have to try it.

Nose breathing, as lightly and slowly as you can, will activate your parasympathetic response and bring you back to flow.

Mouth breathing, by contrast, will activate your sympathetic response.

Your nose is designed to be your body's primary pathway for taking in air. The tiny hairs inside your nostrils both filter and warm the air coming in in a way that the mouth doesn't.

Mouth breathing is more like your body's backup option for when *it just needs air now!* In that way, it's designed for more panicky situations, so breathing through your mouth triggers more of a panicked, sympathetic nervous system response.

Breathe through your nose, lightly and slowly, whenever you can.

I've noticed that elite-level soldiers, for whom performing at their best can determine if they live or die, are constantly using their breath to regulate their nervous systems.

In medieval Japan, samurai were said to have tested a soldier's readiness by placing a feather beneath his nostrils while he inhaled and exhaled. If the feather moved, the soldier would be dismissed: he did not yet possess the nervous system control required to breathe lightly and slowly enough, and thus be grounded and centered enough, to succeed in battle.

Stay grounded and calm, like a samurai

While writing this book, I happened upon the novel *Silent Horizons* by Chad Robichaux, a former Force Recon Marine in the United States army who now writes military thrillers. Throughout the story, Robichaux describes his protagonist Foster Quinn, a Force Recon Marine, re-calibrating his nervous system during intense moments by attending to his breath and heartbeat.

"Nice and slow," Quinn reminds himself as he swims underwater during training at Camp Pendleton, pushing a heavy brick through a pool. "He knew it was counterintuitive to move slowly, [but] the only way he could complete the test was by remaining calm," Robichaux writes.

As Iranian agents threaten to trap and kill Quinn, again he reminds himself, *"Nice and slow,* he thought. Foster's heart rate dipped as he drew a long, slow breath in through his nose." At perhaps ten different points in the book, Foster needs to remind himself to move slower, and breath lightly through his nose, to recalibrate himself into flow.

Try this now: set the timer on your phone to one minute, and focus purely on breathing as lightly and slowly as possible through your nose. Keep the breath continuous—no pauses between inhales and exhales—but as slow as possible. Don't do anything else as you do this. Focus purely on the lightness and slowness of the breath through your nose.

I'm going to do it "with you" right now as I write this.
Ready, set, go.

Has the timer gone off? Hey, I mean it! Really do it!

Ok, how do you feel, having done it?

Having just done the minute myself, I feel a light, airy sensation that's come over my forearms, and a subtle calm overall.

Your experience and sensations are probably different, but of a similar variety.

You can do the light-and-slow-as-possible nose breath anytime, anywhere, for any length of time. It always works.

I've done it while stuck in traffic when I otherwise would have been stressing about showing up late to a talk at a high school that I was scheduled to give. This made sure that I showed up to the talk in parasympathetic, and it went great as a result!

I do it in social settings when a moment of awkward pause arises and it's not quite clear what the next topic of conversation will be. I'd rather tap into my parasympathetic self (1,000x better self!) in that social moment than bury my face in my phone or make up a topic to talk about that I'm not actually wanting to talk about.

In any moment, I want my parasympathetic self—my best self—to be the one who shows up.

I've had students do the light and slow nose breath right when they're about to start their homework, calming the stress that homework brings up for them, and thus enabling them to "glide" into their homework with ease instead of avoiding it and procrastinating.

One student even took himself off of his ADHD medicine by setting a timer and doing parasympathetic breathing every hour, as he did his homework. A couple of my students have raved about how effective the light and slow nose breath was while they took tests.

You'll notice that as you light-and-slow nose breathe your way into parasympathetic, life gets easier to handle. Your natural abilities start to flow through you again—you get to relax—*and* perform way better.

That's what we're here for, right?

"FLOW MOVE" 2: *The 2 Voices Exercise*

Have you noticed? How you talk to yourself is a *massive* factor in your experiencing anxiety versus flow.

Here's a quick exercise that, using your knowledge of the nervous system, will return you to the sanity of parasympathetic's Inner Wisdom voice.

Right when you notice yourself slipping into sympathetic (maybe you notice bodily tension or the Doom and Gloom Voice getting fearful or critical), put into words what each nervous system would say about your situation.

Ask: What is my sympathetic nervous system saying right now? Put it into words: ALL the mean, horrible things it is saying to you right now.

For example, imagine that while passing an acquaintance in the hall at school, you went to say hi, but they looked away. When you put your sympathetic Doom and Gloom Voice into words, it sounds like

> *You idiot! That's so embarrassing! You went to say hi and they ignored you. You're a loser. They're going to laugh about this with their friends. Nobody really likes you...*

Yikes. Now put into words what your parasympathetic Inner Wisdom would say—the honest, compassionate, and wise voice:

> *That was embarrassing! They didn't even respond or say hi back! That hurts. But maybe they didn't see me. Or were distracted. Or having a hard day. I'm not really sure what happened, but however this one person feels about me, it'll be OK in the end.*

Just by putting the two voices into words — which takes five to ten seconds — you'll return to sanity and clarity.

2 Voices

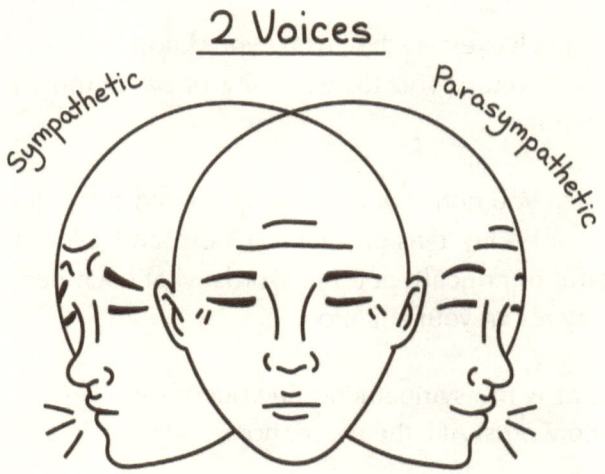

Sympathetic

Parasympathetic

You don't have to *try* to believe the parasympathetic voice. Just hear them both out and relax. It'll be easy to notice what's actually true from there—usually the parasympathetic voice.

And that's one of the amazing things about this. Remember how the sympathetic Doom and Gloom Voice is wrong ninety-nine percent of the time? Your parasympathetic Inner Wisdom voice is *right* ninety-nine percent of the time.

Make a conscious choice to listen to that voice.

The 2 Voices Exercise is ideal for situations where your mental narrative about the situation is running away from you into more and more toxic negativity.

"FLOW MOVE" 3: *Do Annnnnnything Slowwwwly*

Despite all the stress and worry that performance anxiety gives people, it's amazing how simple the topic is underneath it all.

Check out this simple wonder: doing *anything* intentionally more slowly will move you into parasympathetic.

It's that easy.

Try washing your dishes more slowly, or walking to your next class more slowly. Feel your nervous system subtly calm as you do so.

About to walk onstage for a music audition? Take each step onto that stage just a little more slowly than normal. Set yourself up to perform in parasympathetic.

About to take the game-winning foul shots in the high school state championship? Dribble the ball just a little bit slower before taking your shots. Notice how many NBA greats take slow, calming deep breaths right before each foul shot?

Jim Brown, the legendary NFL running back who won three MVPs, used to pick himself up off the ground after every play as slowly as he possibly could. He said he did it to mask to the other team whether or not he was injured, but I also suspect that on some level, he did this habit to reset himself to parasympathetic after every single play.

The great French Formula 1 driver Alain Prost noted that when he moved his hands more slowly to make his turns as he drove, his lap times became quicker.

Over and over, you'll notice that the highest-level performers in any field are *insistent* about taking a moment to choose to move more slowly.

In the Navy Seals, they repeat the mantra during missions, *slow is smooth, and smooth is fast.*

Doesn't this make sense? Your parasympathetic self is your better self. It's your in-flow self. Of course the masters know to slow themselves down when others speed up and get nervous. They're "changing tracks" to a parasympathetic approach to life.

And *that's* why they're masters.

Consider that in almost any film that features a hero, a montage takes place where the character walks extremely slowly, to really cool music, in a moment of huge pressure and stakes?

On a deep level, we all know that the relaxed, parasympathetic version of ourselves is an absolute badass, and it's the badasses who know how to access that version of themselves.

Are you realizing that by the end of this book, *you're* going to be one of those people?

It's a different life path you're about to chart, now that you'll be navigating out of sympathetic and the Doom and Gloom Voice.

Guess how that will shift your confidence.

Well done for reading this far and giving yourself the gift of these awarenesses.

When you reach out to me in the future and tell me what's shown up in your life now that you know how to keep yourself in parasympathetic and flow, you will make my day.

Yes, you're going to send me those emails (info@growthwise.us)!

And yes, your performance in all arenas of life will be forever changed. I can't wait to hear about it from you!

Lily's Story: Volleyball Superstar, Nervous No Longer

An aspiring college volleyball player, Lily met with me during the fall of her high school freshman year. Her club team coach had a habit of yelling at players, and Lily found herself losing confidence, and even her desire to play the sport, amidst her coach's criticism.

"I was just getting very nervous after every mistake," she said, "and always thinking about what my coach was going to say. I would get very overwhelmed."

Once I taught her about her nervous system, though, she realized she'd gotten stuck in a sympathetic nervous system response. Coming from way too far into "succeed at," she began to notice her negative self-talk, and to use the light-and-slow nose breath to move back to parasympathetic.

Since then, she's played the best volleyball of her life. "It's all real!" she told me. "It's actually really helped me improve this season. It's helped me focus more. When I'm in games now, I'm never nervous."

In the past, getting yelled at by her coach would send Lily into a tailspin:

"I would internalize everything, and I would just think I was the worst player on the team. I'd think, 'Oh my God, I'm getting targeted.' I'd think I was the only person getting yelled at, when that's just not the reality. Everyone gets yelled at. It's not just me. I believed that I was the person messing everything up."

Notice how she went from interpreting her coach's yelling in the sympathetic Doom and Gloom Voice (*The coach is targeting me and only me!*) to seeing her coach from the parasympathetic voice of Inner Wisdom (*This happens to everyone. I don't need to worry about it!*)?

Now Lily finds herself coaching her teammates and friends:

"My teammates, compared to last year, they come to me if they need to calm down. Last year, I was already in my own head enough. But people come to me more now and say, 'Ok, what should I do next,' because I've become a lot calmer. They trust me with what I say to them."

Lily's showing up in parasympathetic in school now, too:

"This week, I was taking a math test, and my friend was really nervous, and I was like, 'Ok, I learned this from this guy. You have to breathe in and out your nose really lightly and slowly, and it'll help you get into parasympathetic mode...' I just tell them, 'this is what I learned and it worked for me. So just trust me on this.' And sometimes they do it, and sometimes they don't."

Story of my life, Lily!

More importantly: *well done*!!!

KEY POINTS

CHAPTER 4: FIND FLOW IN PARASYMPATHETIC

The three "Flow Moves" are:

1. Light-and-slow nose breath

2. The 2 Voices exercise—put into words what your sympathetic nervous system voice is saying, and put into words what your para-sympathetic is saying, and then just relax

3. Do Annnnnnything Slowwwwly

The masters in any field know to consciously slow down into their para-sympathetic self, their best self, when others tend to speed up and get nervous.

JOURNAL / REFLECT

CHAPTER 4: FIND FLOW IN PARASYMPATHETIC

1. Where can you use the light-and-slow nose breath in your life? While driving? While taking a test?

2. What's a recent situation where your mental narrative about a situation was making you more and more anxious? Rewind to that moment in your mind and put into words the 2 Voices exercise:

   a. What would your sympathetic nervous system have been saying?

   b. What would your parasympathetic have been saying?

3. What are THREE actions you can consciously do more slowly during a normal week to move yourself into parasympathetic more often?

CHAPTER 5

Performing in Flow!

"It is the highest [LSAT] I've scored. Process was much smoother, and I was much, much faster. I used the breathing practice pretty much constantly throughout the whole test and before I started the third section after my break, I practiced moving a pencil very slowly across my desk. It felt irrelevant whether I got the questions wrong; I was really only focused on understanding the question and then I trusted myself on the answers. Basically, every aspect was significantly improved."

—Toby, formerly anxious LSAT taker

"The test was such a perfect day. [My son] had such a swagger when he came to the car. I said 'Jack, how did you feel?' He said 'Mom, I felt awesome. I had no anxiety, no stress. I did really, really well.' It was an amazing experience."

—Suzanne, parent of a formerly anxious SAT taker

Let's imagine you're a test taker, even if what brought you to this book was a different kind of performance anxiety.

But now, you're going to experience performing with the awareness and habits you've learned from this book.

You know your nervous system and the landscape of "play with" and "succeed at," and you're ready to do things in flow now!

Let's talk about how you prepare for this test, now.

You come home from school or work and see your exam prep materials on your desk. A pang of sympathetic stress hits you.

Old you would have moaned and headed for the kitchen to distract yourself with a snack, then whipped out Tik Tok for an embarrassingly long scroll. An hour would've gone by—where did the time go?!

Scrolling always leaves you feeling empty, and afterwards you *still* don't want to do the exam prep.

You frown and start working on something else. You'll get to studying later that day, you tell yourself (knowing this to be a lie).

But new you is different. You've read this book and know how to stay out of stress: you set a timer for sixty seconds and do the light-and-slow nose breath.

You feel nicely calm. You throw in the 2 Voices exercise because you're a performance anxiety whiz, putting into words what your sympathetic and parasympathetic nervous systems are saying.

> Sympathetic: *I hate this test. It's so stupid. I suck at it. I'm going to fail. Everyone's going to think I'm stupid...*

Already this voice is starting to sound ridiculous to you. Well done.

> Parasympathetic: *Studying isn't that bad, especially when I'm feeling parasympathetic after the light-and-slow nose breath. I'll start now :) I can always stop if it's too much.*

You notice your body feeling more relaxed.

As you glide through your exam prep, you stop every forty-five minutes, setting a short timer, and doing a light-and-slow-as-possible nose breath.

Handling your business is starting to feel easy!

Imagine just about every day between now and the real exam going just like this. Imagine how many more hours of quality studying you're going to put in this way.

You're going to show up to the test better-practiced, more confident, feeling lighter and happier, and even sporting a healthier immune system!

See how far-reaching the effects of staying in parasympathetic and flow are?

Fast forward to test day.

In the past, you'd walk into the exam center, psych yourself out with negative self-talk about your own inferiority compared to other test-takers, and proceed to blank out during the test.

Let's do this differently, now.

You notice stress as you get into your car to drive to the test and immediately stop to set a timer for 30 seconds, so you do the light-and-slow nose breath. Afterwards, you keep the light and slow nose breath going as you drive.

Then you put into words what the sympathetic and parasympathetic nervous systems are saying.

Sympathetic: *Oh God, I'm back here again. I'm going to fail again. The test anxiety book stuff isn't going to work!*

Parasympathetic: *No, you're different now. You know how to stay in parasympathetic all test long. You've been doing it in different parts of your life lately, including on your practice tests, and it always works!*

Your muscles relax as you walk into the exam center. *Wow*, you think: *I'm actually relaxed. This hasn't happened before!* A smile appears on your face.

Isn't *that* student going to stay in flow better on this test than the one you used to be—the one spiraling ever further into too much "succeed at"?

That's the flow formula! Moment after moment, notice if you're slipping into sympathetic, then take yourself back to parasympathetic. Breathe as lightly and slowly as possible through your nose, and do the 2 Voices exercise whenever your mind's voice starts to spin out into catastrophizing.

Find little things you can consciously choose to do more slowly, like walking back into the exam room after the mid-test break.

Notice how much nicer it feels—and how much better you perform—when you get used to constantly recalibrating yourself back from too much "succeed at" and into flow instead.

If your performance anxiety shows up in something outside of tests, like auditions or sports or just plain socializing, it's still the same story.

Notice the tension in your body or the Doom and Gloom Voice speaking, then choose to move back into flow and parasympathetic using any of the three "flow moves."

Decision after decision in your life will get changed to something more in flow now as opposed to more in stress like you used to do.

Look at you now, flow master!

Olivia's Story: From Social Anxiety to Socializing in Flow

Olivia took my ten-week Social Skills for Life course as a high-school freshman.

Before the class, she'd been feeling tremendous anxiety about going to school. She struggled with catty and competitive dynamics at the studio where she danced, and she didn't have the friendships she wanted, either.

One of the things I teach in Social Skills for Life is how to converse with people in a genuine way that puts both you and the person you're speaking to into a parasympathetic state. When neither of you is feeling so anxious and guarded, conversations become really fun and meaningful.

After Social Skills for Life, Olivia found herself feeling grounded and relaxed, connecting with way more people than before, and finding herself in flow socially:

> "It's beautiful to see myself put the tools in action. A couple months ago, I was always trying to fit in, and change myself to become friends with other people. When I did even become friends with other people, it would not be *me* becoming friends with them. It was someone that I was pretending to be. So I would never have that connection with anyone, and I never knew why.
>
> Throughout the past couple weeks and months, I started to make connections that I never thought I would make.
>
> Before, I would always be worried, walking away from conversations feeling like I messed it up and I want to go back and change everything that I said. But now, if I feel like the conversation didn't go well, I appreciate that I even had the guts to go for that conversation.
>
> I love making people feel seen now. It's just amazing! And I love it so much. I love being able to do that for other people."

Life in flow really does feel that good.

*Want these results for your social life and confidence? Check out my classes "Make Them Feel Seen" and "Social Skills for Life" at www.growthwise.us/socialskills. As a thank you for reading this book, use the code **answertoanxious** at checkout for $20 off "Make Them Feel Seen" or **answertoanxious2** for $100 off "Social Skills for Life."]*

KEY POINTS

CHAPTER 5: PERFORMING IN FLOW

No matter whether you're test-taking, playing a sport or instrument, or simply socializing, the flow recipe is the same: Notice yourself slipping into sympathetic (bodily tension, Doom and Gloom Voice in your head), then practice any of the three "flow moves" to come back to flow and parasympathetic.

The only people these moves don't work for are the ones who aren't actually doing them!

JOURNAL / REFLECT

CHAPTER 5: PERFORMING IN FLOW

1. What are THREE parts of your life where you're going to practice the three "flow moves" to bring yourself into flow? Think beyond the part of your life that got you to read this book and see where *else* you can use the tools, too.

CHAPTER 6

Heal the Root Causes of Your Anxiety

"Your work with stress and anxiety was equally or *more* valuable than the test-taking techniques."

—Stacy, mother of a formerly anxious test taker

"I learned a lot about myself because of James. I will use what I learned from him for the rest of my life."

—Athena, formerly anxious test taker

This chapter isn't for everybody, so if you sense it gets a little too deep emotionally or "woo woo," no worries. Stick with the previous chapters and execute what they lay out, and your performance anxiety will be worlds better than when you started this book.

But if you want to resolve the deeper roots of your performance anxiety, so that it stops coming back and you won't even really have to use the three "flow moves" anymore, then this chapter is for you.

As much as I love the three "flow moves" I shared, this chapter is the book's deepest answer to anxious.

It fits closely with the teachings of current-day enlightened spiritual teachers like Michael Singer, Eckhart Tolle, Byron Katie, and many others, not to mention the ancient enlightenment teachings of Buddhism, Hinduism, Daoism, and many other related bodies of knowledge.

To heal the triggers for your anxiety, let's establish what an emotional trigger is: *any emotion you feel in the present moment that doesn't feel like love.*

What is love? Let's define it as a mixture of care, compassion, and an energy of "I see you."

What doesn't feel like love, and thus could be defined as a trigger? Anxiety, sadness, rage, resentment, a feeling of emptiness, etc.

Consider that every time you find yourself feeling triggered, you're in a sympathetic nervous system response, and you're actually acting like a child: irrational, lashing out, exaggerating, overreacting, etc.

The part of you that's feeling triggered is *not* handling things like a calm, grounded adult.

You might be talking to a 61-year-old man, but if he's lashing out at you in rage, then arguably whom you're really speaking to is his 7-year-old self who felt powerless before his own father's rage.

There's a reason we act like children when we're triggered: our triggers come from the emotional wounds of our childhoods. Most of our wounds root back to when we were kids, when we were most vulnerable and emotionally wound-able.

We might've been traumatized by an abusive boss in our 20s, but the reason that boss bothered us so deeply could have been because of bullying we experienced from older kids in our neighborhood when we were six.

See how emotional wounds can link back to each other across the timelines of our lives?

Now notice this: different people get triggered by different things. Your socially awkward friend gets triggered by meeting new people, but he calmly aces his exams at school, while a socially-relaxed friend blanks out each time he takes a test.

What determines your triggers? The particular emotionally wounding experiences of your past, ninety-nine percent of which you've probably forgotten, consciously at least.

But your subconscious remembers *everything* you've experienced.

Most of us don't remember each of the particular experiences that created our triggers, but that doesn't make them any less present in our subconscious.

You know what would have healed these wounds right when they happened, and prevented them from becoming a trigger you carry with you for the rest of your life?

If somebody had been there to lovingly acknowledge your experience, your pain—to be there with you and let you know they see and care and have compassion for what you were going through.

Something about loving compassion has a way of making pain dissolve.

When someone shows up to us that way, our pain digests and integrates. We learn lessons from the experience, but we're free to move on, too, unburdened by what happened.

Every child wishes they had a figure like the grandfather in the picture below to make them feel cared about and seen each time they felt pain.

More often than not, though, the people around us when we were young *weren't* able to give us that level of emotional support. Often they weren't around, so we were literally alone with our pain. Other times, even when they were there with us, they still made us feel alone: by not noticing that we were hurting, or by seeming unable to understand us, or by shaming us for having a big emotional response to something that they, as adults, considered trivial.

All of these responses make a child feel alone with their pain.

When we feel alone with our pain, it tends to overwhelm us, driving us to try to suppress or dissociate from it. Those responses are what end up storing our pain in our subconscious, compelling us thereafter to toxic behaviors like abuse or addiction.

Meanwhile, having someone there to lovingly witness our pain, particularly when we are kids, is life-changingly powerful. Psychologist Marc Brackett founded the Yale Center for Emotional Intelligence, and he specializes in this very topic.

In a podcast interview with Whitney Goodman, "Do You Have an Uncle Marvin?" Brackett describes an "Uncle Marvin" as a trusted, loving adult who "created the conditions for you [as a kid] to feel safe and comfortable to talk about feelings, and provided that emotional support."

Brackett's surveys suggest only one-third of people had someone like that in their childhood.

While repressing pain in the moment can help us get through an elementary school day full of bullying, or a stressful meal with family members fighting, it comes at a cost: dissociating from painful feelings leaves emotional triggers in our subconscious.

Whenever future experiences subconsciously remind us of that original experience, we get activated into sympathetic: heart beating faster, breath becoming shallow, and the voice in our head sounding critical, fearful, and mean (Doom and Gloom).

That's what triggers feel like. And man, they're strong and fast when they hit, aren't they?

We barely know what happened when suddenly we're flooded with fear, rage, or sadness.

Remember how I mentioned that if someone had known how to lovingly be there with us (an "Uncle Marvin") when we were hurt as kids, the wound would have healed and wouldn't have gotten stored inside our subconscious as a trigger?

That is the insight we use to heal our old triggers.

You might be wondering how you can heal a wound now that took place so long ago.

Well, a key aspect of human emotion is that *the subconscious does not know time*. In the subconscious, our past and present are *always* happening. They aren't separate! Consider post traumatic stress disorder (PTSD): an Iraq war veteran who served twenty years ago may suffer panic attacks when he's around fireworks or intense thunder now in 2025, since they remind him of traumatic explosions he experienced in battle in 2005.

In PTSD, it's like the past is happening right now. That's because in that person's psyche, the past *is* happening right now.

It's the same with our emotional triggers. Triggers are like tiny moments of emotional PTSD—moments of pain that got repressed instead of lovingly acknowledged, and thus they got stored in our psyche.

Since the subconscious thinks that when we're triggered we're living in the time of the original wounding, *that means we can lovingly acknowledge that wound now*, and heal it.

When we feel a trigger like anxiety in the present moment, we can be the "Uncle Marvin" to ourselves that we needed, but didn't have, in the past.

That's what I'm going to show you how to do. To heal any triggers coming up in the moment,

STEP 1: Notice What Isn't a Feeling of Love

Ask yourself any moment: is there anything I'm feeling right now that *isn't* a feeling of love?

Are you feeling a little anxiety, or maybe a little resentment, from an interaction you had an hour ago? Maybe you're feeling sad, or stressed—you get the idea. Anything right now that doesn't feel like love is a trigger from your past.

For me as I write this, I'm feeling quite full of love—blessed to be as much in parasympathetic as I am, writing a book I'm so passionate about.

But I can sense, let's say, a four percent background amount of anxiety: something about getting this writing done before embarking on the subsequent things I have to do today.

So that four percent anxiety stems from emotional wounds in my past. Do I *need* to be experiencing anxiety about things I have to

---

do later today? No. Is it possible to be purely in flow right now as I write this book, and to still flow to my other activities I'm going to do later today, without any stress? Of course it is. Plenty of people on this planet are flowing through their day's activities exactly like that, taking care of whatever they have to, without any stress.

Do I know which experiences caused this anxiety? No. I've forgotten ninety-nine percent of them. But I know that I spent *years* feeling like I was never doing enough, that I always had to do things better than I was doing them (thanks, Doom and Gloom Voice!).

That was a constant, emotionally wounding way to be with myself, so it's no wonder I still have triggers like them lingering inside.

STEP 2: Notice Where the Triggered Energy Lives in Your Body

After noticing what emotion you're experiencing that doesn't feel like love, close your eyes and notice where this energy seems to live in your body.

For the anxiety I'm experiencing right now, I notice it in my temples beside my eyes, primarily, and a little bit in the middle of my chest.

Where do you notice *your* feelings that don't feel like love, in this moment?

Wherever the triggered energy lives in your body…

STEP 3: Bring Patient Compassion to the Trigger

This is the "Uncle Marvin" move: imagine an adult lovingly being with a kid who's in pain, maybe putting into words with care what the kid is feeling (e.g. "you feel so hurt," or "you wanted to be invited to that party so badly—that makes sense"), and just sitting with them while the kid feels listened to and cared about.

That's how you're going to show up to your own emotional trigger in the moment right now. Bring your attention to where you feel the trigger in your body, the feeling that doesn't feel like love, and just be with it, lovingly.

Some people like to imagine wrapping the energy of the trigger in calming pink or blue light inside your body—you can get creative here.

Or maybe just imagine being with your trigger—really your younger, wounded self—the same way the grandfatherly figure in the image above is being with his hurt grandson.

Close your eyes and bring this loving, space-holding awareness to your emotional trigger… until your mind wanders or you get bored. It could take anywhere from five to sixty seconds, say.

Try it right now. Re-read the previous page if you need to, and try it.

How do you feel afterwards?

Notice that the trigger has lightened, and you feel a little more parasympathetic than before?

Sometimes when people do this step, they notice their attention wandering and then try to will themselves back to focusing on the pain. You don't need to do this. Once your mind wanders, even if it's after just five seconds, your healing meditation for this moment is done.

That short time bringing loving awareness to your pain is enough for now. When the trigger comes back, you'll get to do it again.

Each healing meditation is like a little step of growth, maturity, and progress.

Think of this: you could have a piece of fish for dinner tonight, and that's a perfect amount to eat. As healthy as fish is, eating ten pounds of it wouldn't be healthy! Your body can't process that much.

Your mind and heart can only process so much pain at a time, too. So once your mind wanders, think of that as the signal that this short, healing meditation you just did is complete.

You'll get plenty of chances to be with and heal this pain more. Some wounds, especially the deeper ones, you'll come back to tens or even hundreds of times, and that's OK. Those are wounds you probably experienced over and over in the past.

The wounds that trigger us are like onions, with many layers, and each little healing meditation is another layer of the onion getting removed. Keep at it, and in time, this wound will entirely disappear, and you won't have this trigger anymore.

The anxiety you feel in certain situations can entirely disappear this way.

STEP 4: Don't Try to *Change* the Triggered Feeling

Just keep a loving attention on it. The trigger will dissipate by itself. Your job isn't to change the feeling. It's only to love it.

There's a certain way we want to be with our pain when we bring our attention to it: patiently, lovingly, and compassionately—the same way we wish someone had been with us when we were hurting as kids.

When teaching this to clients, I notice two mistakes that they make when they're first learning it, causing it not to work.

First, they bring compassionate attention to the pain *with the intention of making the pain go away.* They're trying to change the pain into a different feeling.

But have you ever been upset and had someone tell you to relax, or that you're overreacting, and try to coach you into feeling something different? It didn't work, right? It made you even more infuriated!

The pain we carry feels the same: it doesn't want you to rush it, or resolve it, or change it. It just wants you to be with it, lovingly and patiently.

Remember: that trigger is your wounded younger self inside. It is a being in its own right, a version of you from some point in your past. Like anyone else, it doesn't want to be changed out of its feelings: it just wants to be loved where it is.

The second mistake I see people make with this process is to *dive into the pain.* They try to *feel* it, intensely.

You don't need to *immerse* yourself in your anxiety. Just *be with* it, lovingly.

When my clients *become* the trigger, the meditation never ends. It goes on for several minutes!

But we aren't trying to *become* the rage or the sadness or the fear; that's just you becoming the wounded child again. We're trying to be with the pain, compassionately, like a loving adult would.

In this process, we're showing up as the adult in parasympathetic—holding space, giving the pain as long as it needs to just be. Paradoxically, this posture makes the pain process quickest, in my experience.

Some people find that it works to imagine wrapping the pain in a hug or even whispering to the trigger in their minds' voice, "You make sense. I'm here with you. I see you." See what feels like *your* style of showing love to your pain.

STEP 5: Notice How Much Lighter You Feel Now

You just healed an emotional wound you were carrying, a part of your emotional patterning, from a sympathetic to a parasympathetic response.

You'll find that the next time you face the situation that triggered you, you will be less triggered than you used to be! The more times you do these meditations, the less and less triggered you'll feel, until finally you won't feel triggered at all. Instead, you'll feel calm, loving, and confident instead.

Believe me!

I've seen this happen in countless areas of my life, enabling me to be *so* much less anxious that I used to be. As effective as the three "flow moves" from chapter four are for situations, bringing loving awareness to your triggers is the deepest answer to anxious.

Further Thoughts

1. Three years of practice

The teacher I learned this trigger-healing meditation from, Greg Paul, says it takes about three years of consistent daily practice of healing one's triggers to the point where you're basically un-triggerable.

Having done it myself, I can see that to be true. I am remarkably less triggerable than I used to be. I feel like a new and different person—more and more of the person I always wanted to be. More relaxed, confident, loving, humble, at ease, and in love with life.

I stop and do a trigger healing meditation ten to forty times per day—any moment I notice a trigger coming up and can stop briefly to do the meditation, I do—oftentimes they only last a few seconds.

2. You can heal triggers inside of you ahead of time, before a particular situation is likely to trigger you!

Think ahead to your next exam, public speaking opportunity, or sports match when your coach is likely to yell at you again.

Imagine what triggered emotions you're likely to feel in that situation. Anger? Fear? Anxiety?

Notice where those triggered emotions live in your body.

You guessed what's next: bring patient, loving, compassionate attention to that trigger. If you already know a situation's going to trigger you in the future, then that trigger exists inside of you already, and you can heal it now. Keep that loving attention on the triggered energy in your body until your mind wanders or you become bored.

Notice how much lighter you feel? Notice the shift into parasympathetic you just experienced?

Well done :) You're a little more healed now than you were before.

Keep doing this leading up to that event, and I guarantee your experience will be less triggered, and way better, than it's ever been.

---

3. Wherever you have wounds and triggers inside you, they will act as magnets, drawing the same problems and dramas to you over and over again.

More and more, I've come to see people as manifesting machines, magnetizing the same things to ourselves over and over.

Ever notice how certain people attract the same types of drama over and over again? Your friend who can't take authority from your sports coach can't take authority from his teachers, either. Over and over, this friend finds authority figures who trigger him into anxiety, disrespectful behavior, or rage, and things get uncomfortable for everyone involved.

Until you heal them, the wounds you have inside will continually attract experiences that make you feel the same triggered emotions over and over again.

It's as if the universe is putting you through the same challenge until you finally learn the lesson: to heal the pain in your heart that those earlier wounding experiences first put there.

Here's the thing: once you heal your triggers and wounds, you stop manifesting those dramas.

Instead of you showing up from old triggers, you show up from a feeling of love instead.

And from that place of love, instead of manifesting your fears and wounds, *you begin to manifest your dreams and desires instead.*

You start to play that instrument the way you always wanted to play it, without the stress. You show up in your sport with the grace and confidence you always yearned to play with. You attract the friends and the partner that you always dreamed of having but couldn't seem to find before.

Try it out. Give the practice three months. See if this doesn't start to come true for you.

And then my advice, of course, will be to keep going!

4. Wherever you're speaking or acting from a trigger, you're hurting the people around you.

This can be a hard one to stomach, because most of us are acting from triggers to some degree nearly all of the time. But it's true.

When you speak or act from anger, the edge in your voice is hurtful to whoever is on the receiving end.

When you speak or act from anxiety, your words tend to hurt the situation rather than help it.

When you become absorbed in your own anxiety, the people around you feel the pain of your absent presence. They're dying to connect with you.

Think of a person you know who carries a lot of stress, and imagine all of that stress just *vanishing* one day—a relaxed, bright, loving person left in their wake. How *good* does that feel to be around them now?

That version of ourselves is whom we're robbing other people of getting to be around, so long as our triggers are still running our show.

When I realized this, I began to apologize anytime I noticed I'd spoken or acted from a trigger. It didn't matter how right I was in the argument, or how wrong the other person was in what they'd said or done to me—if I have a trigger, I can heal that, so it's my responsibility to.

There are people in this world who, no matter what you say or do to them, can respond to you from a feeling of love, absent of any triggers. If they can do it, so can we. We just have some triggers in the way to heal before we get to that place.

It's also my responsibility to *stop* myself from speaking or acting from a trigger. I need to separate myself from triggering situations, and calm my nervous system, before speaking or acting, so I can avoid hurting the people in my life.

Remember: your parasympathetic self is 1,000x better at life than your sympathetic self!

My Story: Healing Triggers to Turn a New Page with Family

I was going to tell the story here of stepping onstage in Los Angeles at The Moth, the world's premier storytelling venue, and entering a storytelling competition despite having never told a story onstage before.

In short, I used the healing meditation in the day before the event to de-trigger any performance anxiety I could, and it worked great.

But I have a more meaningful experience to share instead.

I come from a family where my parents and two older brothers are markedly different from me. I always felt like the black sheep, and I had emotional wounds around feeling unheard, misunderstood, and judged by them.

For the last two decades, when I would return home to visit, they would tighten in fear that I was about blow up at them yet again over our differences. Needless to say, I didn't handle my triggers well.

But the trigger healing meditation in this chapter changed me. During my first visit home after two months of practicing these meditations, I stayed with my parents for five days and didn't get into a single fight with them. That had never happened before.

I'd still sometimes run into the differences I'd always felt with my family, but when that happened and it caused me sadness or resentment, I'd bring love to my pain until it passed.

A few months later, I visited my parents again for a week, and at the end of that week, my dad and I sat in the TV room together. We talked quietly and enjoyed each other's presence in a more peaceful way than I ever remember doing. At times we shared honestly about hard issues between us, the ones that would have turned into a fight in the past, but the vibration between us was different now.

"You seem so relaxed!" he said all of a sudden. "It's like a switch has been flipped inside you."

"I know," I answered. "I don't need you guys to understand me anymore, and I don't need to coach you or dump my beliefs on you anymore, either."

He laughed. "You don't!"

After an embarrassingly long number of years, a page had finally turned. Years of flare-ups and bitterness over our differences have softened into a peaceful acceptance, a relinquishing of old arguments, and a sense of humor about it all.

As powerful as it is to resolve performance anxiety, healing rifts with family hits at a level even deeper and sweeter.

KEY POINTS

CHAPTER 6: HEAL THE ROOT CAUSES

Here are the five steps of the trigger-healing meditation:

1. Ask: Is there anything I'm feeling right now that isn't a feeling of love? That's your trigger in that moment.

2. Close your eyes. Find in your body where the energy of trigger lives.

3. Bring patient, compassionate attention to this pain in this part of your body. Simply be with it until you get bored or your mind wanders.

4. Make sure not to try to rush the process, or to change the feeling. Just be with it lovingly—it will change itself. It's not your job to change it. It's your job to love it.

5. Notice how much lighter you feel afterwards. You just moved a part of your emotional body from a sympathetic to parasympathetic response, permanently.

Do this as many times per day as you can. Greg Paul says it takes three years of consistently practicing it, day by day, to become un-triggerable in your life.

Use the healing meditations to de-trigger yourself *before* a predictably triggering event that's coming up for you.

Where you still have wounds and triggers, you'll manifest the same dramas and emotions, over and over. Once you heal them, you begin to manifest your dreams and desires, instead.

When you speak or act from a trigger, you will hurt others. Stop yourself when you're triggered (remove yourself from the situation if you have to), calm your nervous system, use the healing meditation in this chapter, and *then* speak or act. This is hard to do, but an absolute game-changer for your life.

JOURNAL / REFLECT

CHAPTER 6: HEAL THE ROOT CAUSES

1. Check in right now: what might you be feeling that's not a feeling of love? What percentage of your emotions right now would you say that feeling makes up– twenty, five, or maybe fifty? Run through the five steps and see if that triggered emotion hasn't dissipated by the end of it.

2. Where do you notice you tend to feel triggers in your life *outside* of performance anxiety?

3. What's a situation that's coming up where you're likely to feel triggered—something other than a feeling of love—and can you do five healing meditations on those triggers right now, before the event takes place? Notice how much more relaxed you feel when that situation comes around.

CONCLUSION

The Spirit of Flow

"James has totally changed my perspective on life. I have all around become a much happier person and greatly due to everything he has taught me. It is funny to explain to my friends that the anecdotes I often share came from my ACT tutor. I am so grateful for all the skills I have learned from him. Thank you, James, for teaching me to have trust in myself."

—Hannah, formerly anxious test taker

"I really wanted to just thank you, James. Our classes were always about the SAT but from all these breathing techniques, life outlooks, and stories about people who have improved their lives with an outlook, I've been able to improve not just my score in the SAT but also myself. I really appreciate this new form that you have molded teaching into."

—Jack, formerly anxious test taker

This conclusion will seem even further outside the box than the last chapter. You're going to think, "Why are you talking about this stuff, tutor guy? It doesn't even make sense! Stay in your lane!!"

Easy, dear reader!

You can drop the book here, practice the slow-and-light-as-possible nose breath, 2 Voices exercise, and do-annnnnnything-slowly techniques, and waltz your way to flow and parasympathetic for the rest of your life. If that's what happens, then this book has done its job.

And if you're using the trigger-healing meditation too, goodness, you're on your way to an amazing life.

You can stop here. But, if you can't help yourself from indulging your crazy author in a *spiritual* conversation about performance anxiety and flow, then read on.

In the Christian tradition, Jesus spoke of aligning with the Holy Spirit ("I and the Father are one" John 10:30). The enlightened Chinese philosopher Laozi wrote about becoming one with the Dao, while Chinese medicine speaks of *qi*. In Japan, they call it *reiki*. In the Hindu tradition, it's *prana*. In the current day western scientific tradition, we call it "energy."

All of these cultures and traditions are speaking about the same thing: the energy that flows through our universe—an energy so omnipresent and all-encompassing that you could call it divine.

There's energy flowing through you and me right now, of course: in the train of thoughts you're having as you read this book, or in the emotions you've been experiencing over the course of the last hour.

Energy flows emerge in every part of life: changing weather, cultural trends, or the direction your favorite TV show took last season.

Even the bed in your room, stationary as it seems, is said by physicists to be made up of atoms that are constantly vibrating and moving. *Everything* in this universe is energy, and energy has a vibration and flow to it.

When we relax and allow the energy flowing through us to come through, unblocked by our triggers or fears, THAT is the "flow" of peak performance.

It's where all of our gifts come out to play.

All the different kinds of intelligence that we have inside— academic intelligence, athletic intelligence, artistic intelligence, etc.—get expressed when we align with the energy that wants to come through us.

Notice how much better of an athlete, or a friend, or a test taker you become when you're relaxed and in flow?

THAT is you at your best. And you cannot access flow in sympathetic. Fear, shame, the Doom and Gloom Voice—they all *block* your flow.

So the more you get yourself into parasympathetic—the more you relax your body and release the critical, fearful, and mean voice that wants to restrict you, not to mention the emotional wounds of your past that sit like triggers inside you—the more you come into flow—the more you allow your God-given gifts to be expressed.

You know that moment when you do something so good that you can't even believe it?

You pull a move in practice or a game that you've never done before, or you tell a joke so good you even surprise yourself with how funny it was?

Those are the *best* moments in life, aren't they? We revel in them, reminisce over them, and *hope* others notice and comment.

Those are moments of flow, when you got out of sympathetic and allowed your intelligence to show itself.

The reason you were showing up at such a high level in those moments is because *it wasn't you who did that*—it was a higher power that you allowed to flow through you.

When Jesus spoke of the Holy Spirit or Laozi wrote of the Dao, they were describing a higher, much greater power than themselves or any other individual.

This is what athletes like Lionel Messi and Steph Curry, arguably the greatest in their respective sports, are referencing when they celebrate having just done something amazing on the field or court.

Messi and Curry celebrate in *the exact same way*: they hit their chests (the heart, considered by most major religions to be our access point to God) and then point to the sky as if to say, "You did that, God, not me. You came through me, and I am just your channel. Thank you."

But you cannot channel the divine—you cannot allow this greater flow and intelligence to course through you—unless you relax and remove the blocks.

And because Messi and Curry know a higher power is executing the brilliance that just came through them, they know to simply get out of the way and humbly appreciate what comes through.

That is their answer to anxious. These two guys seem to know a thing or two about performing at the highest level.

Why am I telling you all of this?

Because you, dear reader, are a much greater being than you know.

There is an intelligence wanting to come through you that you've only glimpsed in moments so far in your life. It is so much greater than you realize.

You've probably been living in your sympathetic nervous system about seventy-five to ninety percent of the last several years. Think of how many hours that adds up to, where the critical, fearful, and mean Doom and Gloom Voice has been the one talking to you.

You didn't know about your nervous system yet, so you tended to believe what the Doom and Gloom Voice told you!

Your self esteem and self-love are nowhere near as high as they deserve to be.

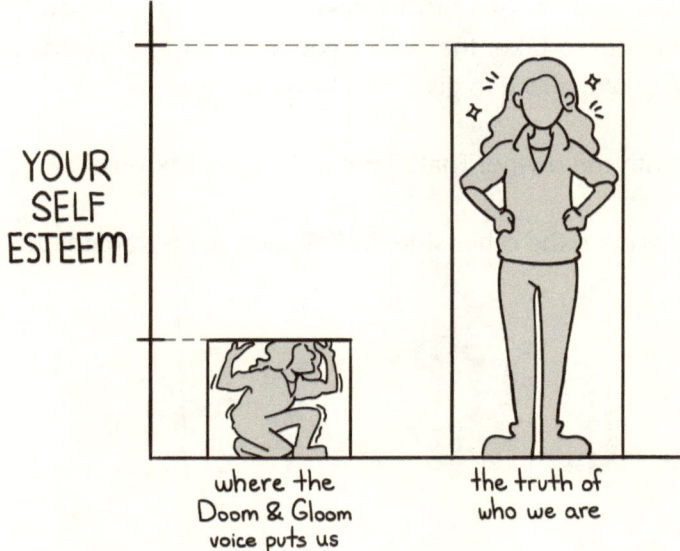

YOUR
SELF
ESTEEM

where the
Doom & Gloom
voice puts us

the truth of
who we are

As long as you've been in sympathetic, you've been blocking this intelligence that wants to come through—to express the unique person and gifts that you are.

YOU are a gift. Nobody tells a joke, or chooses an outfit, or strings together information, or expresses joy or love, quite like you do. Nobody else brings the flavor to this life that you do.

But you cannot express the intelligence wanting to come through you when your body is tight, your mind is full of fear, shame, or criticism, and you're blocking flow.

So, step into flow. Join me here! It is magical. The gifts that will begin to express through you will surprise you and those around, and maybe all you'll be able to do is point to the sky with thanks.

That is your birthright.

With the awarenesses of this book, you're ready — on the test you're about to take, the match you're about to play, the performance you're about to give, and beyond.

Align with the divine. That's your answer to anxious.

I'll see you on the other side, in flow and parasympathetic.

A NOTE FROM ME TO YOU

Thank you so much for spending time with this book's insights, all of which took at least twenty years, and $1.5 million of my own earnings spent on coaching and seminars, to arrive at.

They've changed my life, and I hope they can do the same for you, much quicker than it took me!

If you'd like to work with me personally, send me an email at info@growthwise.us. In addition to performance anxiety for students, athletes, and artists, I specialize in raising people's social skills, be they teenagers looking to make better friends or parents wanting to reconnect with their teen.

Finally, I would *love* to hear your questions, feedback, and success stories. Reach out to me. I can't wait to hear about the ever-more-brilliant version of you who gets to show up in this world.

Excited by the flow coming our way!

—James

ABOUT THE AUTHOR

James Treadway graduated with de-
grees from Harvard College ('08),
Peking University ('10), and the Lon-
don School of Economics ('11) before
deciding that resolving the anxiety
that defined those years was more
important than pursuing further the
fields he had studied. He founded
the tutoring company Growth Wise
in 2013 and proceeded to become a
widely-referred expert among other
tutors as the go-to for students struggling with test anxiety. In
2023, he launched "Social Skills for Life," an online course designed to help teenagers struggling with social anxiety, as well.
He also coaches parents on how to reconnect with their teen by
making them feel seen and heard. *Answer to Anxious* is James'
first book, and he's itching to pen many more!

www.growthwise.us
www.growthwise.us/socialskills
info@growhtwise.us
IG: @socialskillsforlife
IG: @growthwise

APPENDIX

Further reflections on sympathetic and parasympathetic nervous system responses

By now you know how important it is to stay in parasympathetic. This appendix shares further thoughts so you can root yourself even more deeply there.

Are Your Daily and Weekly Habits Bringing Out Your Parasympathetic Nervous System?

Do you feel like a generally anxious person? Even if you don't, look at the following list of activities, all of which will bring out your parasympathetic self. Consider how many of them you do regularly, and which ones you could do a bit more of, so that you can be your parasympathetic self an even higher percentage of your time.

- **Yoga, Meditation, Tai Chi, etc.** - Any mindfulness-based practice is designed to move you into a parasympathetic state. No wonder you feel so light, relaxed, and rested after these activities. As I once heard the billionaire comedian Jerry Seinfeld say (someone whom I always admired for how relaxed and present he seemed onscreen), "I don't care who you are. Being a human being is hard. If you're not taking care of your nervous system, you're stupid." Seinfeld has meditated every day since 1972, and he says he never could have put on a show as big as *Seinfeld* without his 20-minute meditation during lunchtime every day.

- **Prayer** - If you have a religious or spiritual relationship with God, then prayer will put you into a more parasympathetic state. You might find it interesting that the rhythms, cadences, and even geometries of the physical spaces in religious settings all seem designed to calm and relax the mind into a more parasympathetic state. In parasympathetic, we connect to a higher power.

- **Exercise, Dance, Sports, an Undistracted Walk** - ANYTHING that moves your body will put you into a more parasympathetic state afterwards. While most workouts put you into a sympathetic state *during* the workout, afterwards you'll settle into a deeply parasympathetic state. That calm, good feeling you have after a run, workout, or sports practice? That's what we're aiming for.

- **Nature** - Be it skiing, hiking, going to the beach, or just taking a walk and appreciating the birds, wind, and trees, being in nature will move you into a parasympathetic state. Being in nature isn't just a nice idea—it's imperative to optimal health.

- **Water** - My grandfather grew up a poor kid during the Great Depression, and his lifelong mental health advice, for any issue, was simple: "Go take a shower." And he was right! Whether it's a shower, bath, or going swimming, immersing yourself in water will always move you into parasympathetic. In my (highly anxious) twenties, I found myself called to take a bath each night, and every time I came out feeling like a new, refreshed person.

- **Being with *people* who make you feel parasympathetic** - Think about a group of people and then ask: do you feel like you can be your authentic self around them? Or will they judge or make fun of you if you show your true colors? People with whom you feel supported and appreciated for being your unique self are parasympathetic in their effect on you. People who make you feel you have to hide parts of yourself to avoid criticism or judgment are sympathetic in their effect. If you're wondering how to find friends who truly support and appreciate your authentic self, consider my twelve-week Social Skills for Life class which I teach on Zoom: **www.growthwise.us/ socialskills**.

- **Reading and Making Art (Drawing, Painting, Playing an Instrument, etc.)** - These hobbies bring me so much joy, and I've learned that I NEED to carve out space for them in my daily routine in order to feel truly fulfilled in my life. Of course they both put me into a parasympathetic state.

- **Video Games and Social Media Scrolling** - You were hoping I'd put these here! Sadly, they do NOT tend to leave you feeling relaxed and refreshed afterwards. During them, yes, you'll feel parasympathetic, but afterwards you'll tend to feel regret and *more* stress. Finding yourself doing WAY too much of these two activities? Check out the following piece on addictions and "sticky" behaviors...

Addictions, "Sticky" Behaviors, and Your Sympathetic Nervous System

Do you have "sticky" relationships with any behaviors that you know are not good for you, yet you find yourself engaging in them more than you'd like? Perhaps especially when you're feeling stressed?

For some of us, it's social media scrolling, video games, or You-Tube watching. For others it's excessive snacking or engaging in state-altering substances like marijuana, vaping, alcohol, etc.

What all of these behaviors have in common is that they are people's instinctive way of fleeing the discomfort of a stressed, sympathetic nervous system response.

Before we know how to move ourselves into parasympathetic by ourselves, we go to our addiction because it's the only thing we can rely on to ease us out of stress.

But the stress always comes back. Once that candy bar is eaten or you finally extract yourself from that social media scroll, the stress floods right back. Except now you also feel ashamed for having engaged in the behavior that you know isn't good for you!

Once you've learned to move yourself into parasympathetic on your own, you'll find you don't need those addictive habits anymore.

Feel the urge to indulge? Set your phone timer for sixty seconds and do a light-and-slow nose-breathe, then make your choice to engage in the activity or not.

You can still go onto social media or eat unhealthy food, but you get to make that choice from parasympathetic—the wiser

---

you—who knows there's a time and a place for those things without overindulging in them.

Here's the experience of one of my addiction clients Jessica, whom I only needed to see once on Zoom to share this book's insights about the nervous system and her "sticky" relationship with marijuana:

> "Hi James! I wanted to reach out to you because my heart is so full of gratitude. I feel like I'm on the other side of the addiction. I feel like I've come home to myself. Like it's safe to be here and I have no desire to numb. Thank you for holding space for me and pouring into me the way you did. It was just what I needed to shift this!"

Procrastination and Your Sympathetic Nervous System

Do you struggle with procrastination? Yup, it's rooted in stress and a sympathetic response!

Due to past experiences, work may cause you stress: feelings of not being smart enough or productive enough, let's say. Or maybe it was just that schoolwork always took you away from more fun things to do!

At the same time, you know that feeling of pride that you get after you've scored well on a test or done an assignment well? As a tutor, I could tell in the first few seconds of a session with a student how well they did on the homework I'd assigned them, based purely on their posture and tone of voice in the first thing they said. The feeling of pride in a job well done was palpable.

We need that pride in our accomplishments to feel good about ourselves, in my opinion, whether we're ready to admit it or not.

So next time you find yourself putting off your work when you know you SHOULD probably be starting on it, get yourself into parasympathetic first.

Set a timer and do the light-and-slow nose breath for sixty seconds, say. Do the 2 Voices exercise to see what your sympathetic and parasympathetic nervous systems are saying about doing some work right now.

You could use the trigger healing meditation, too.

Once you're in parasympathetic, *now* make your choice about what to do next. You might still decide to relax and enjoy yourself! That's OK! But make your choice from parasympathetic. That's

---

your 1,000x better self. And remember: your parasympathetic mind's voice tells the truth.

There's a time and a place for the hard stuff in life—the challenges, the stuff that has to get done. Your parasympathetic knows when to relax, and it knows when to take care of business, while your sympathetic only knows how to run away from work or to stress about it.

Stay in parasympathetic and it'll handle your work way better than your stressed self ever did.

Why So Many Seem Stuck in Sympathetic Nowadays

If you notice you're always in sympathetic, don't feel bad. Most people are.

Consider this: over the roughly three million years that humans and our ancestors have spent on Earth, we spent that time almost entirely in smaller hunter-gatherer tribes, hanging out in nature, surrounded by loved ones we knew and trusted, with plenty of time to relax when we weren't hunting.

Not until 10,000 years ago did agriculture begin to arrive, humans stopped roaming nomadically, and cities and towns began to emerge. That's only 0.3% of our existence on earth!

So in the 99.7% of humans' time on earth spent living as hunter-gatherers in small tribes, besides moments of extreme stress (war, disease, being chased by a predator), we probably spent *much* larger swaths of our time compared to today in a para-sympathetic state: enjoying nature, singing and dancing, playing sports, etc. Ever notice that just being in nature tends to put us into a healthy, parasympathetic state? That's where we used to spend all our time!

Parasympathetic used to be our natural way of being.

In today's society, however, stress and sympathetic rule the day: we're bombarded with fear messaging by media and social media ("if it bleeds, it leads" they purportedly say in the news business); we spend our time indoors in our rooms or offices or in cars instead of in nature; we have rude and unpleasant interactions with strangers we'll never see again, who feel no obligation to treat us well; and we're consistently told by peers or media that we should be wealthier, more attractive, more productive, more successful, etc. Meanwhile, many of us spend most of each week engaging in school or careers that we don't like and aren't interested in, yet feel forced to do!

In other words, in almost every way, today's way of life suffers from profound alienation and anxiety. We're constantly being pushed into a sympathetic nervous system response. So don't be too hard on yourself if you usually find yourself in a stressed state.

Some of the incentives behind *keeping* a populace stuck in a sympathetic state, meanwhile, might be worth considering. When we're stuck in sympathetic, we easily develop mental and physical health problems, not to mention addictions. Think about how much money various industries make through pharmaceutical drugs, for example, or the foods and other substances that people, out of their anxiety, become addicted to? We're talking about profits in the trillions of dollars, probably!

Meanwhile, from a "controlling the population" standpoint, know that when we're in a sympathetic nervous system state, we can't process conflicting information very well. Think about trying to convince a friend of something when they were stressed: it was like nothing could get into their brain, no matter how much sense you made.

Across history, government has had an incentive to push whatever narrative onto the population would most support its interests. Meanwhile, when people feel scared, they tend to look for authority figures to tell them what to do and how to think. Authority figures can consolidate their power over a population by keeping them frightened and blaming various "bad guys" for people's troubles.

It's sad but possibly true: there may be numerous powerful forces in society that don't want us to be connected to our parasympathetic self. They'd rather keep us anxious, scared, and weakened—but that doesn't mean we have to let them win the battleground of our nervous systems.

I believe our nervous systems *are* a battleground, whether we realize it or not, and our ability to live the lives of our own choosing, as our very best selves, depends on our habits and skill in regulating our nervous systems as we journey through this life.

Now that you know what you know, *you* get to take your nervous system back into the parasympathetic state that will serve you best.

And yes, you'll find some addictive habits disappearing, and your feet more likely to march to the beat of your own drum.

Ignorance of the Menstrual Cycle
Keeps Women Trapped in Sympathetic

For female readers, I cannot recommend Alexandra Pope and Sjanie Wurlitzer's book on the menstrual cycle *Wild Power* highly enough. It highlights how society fails to support women in their cycles, and certainly not to have a parasympathetic experience of this process. Stuck in ignorance about the deeper workings of the menstrual cycle by a society that doesn't teach them, women frequently find themselves in a stressful and very sympathetic experience of their cycle instead. The authors guide women on how to honor their cycle and extract themselves from the stress trap that menstruation can become for them. The picture they paint of a menstrual cycle experienced in parasympathetic is breathtaking.

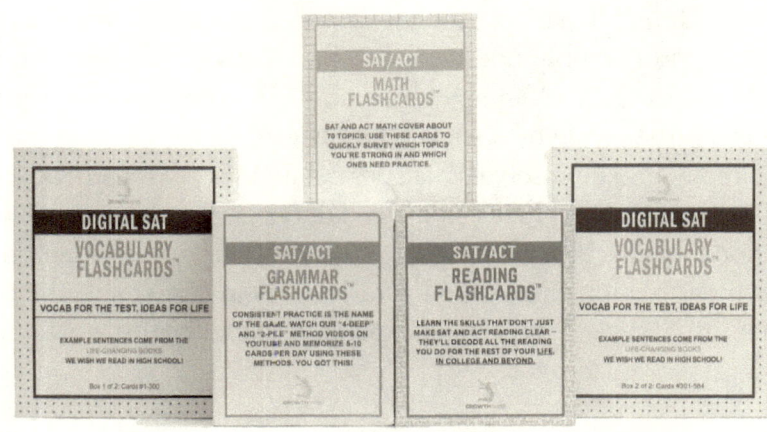

STUDYING FOR THE SAT OR ACT?

James' tutoring company Growth Wise produces SAT and ACT flashcards that put everything you need to know for each section of the test into one place: a box of distraction-free flashcards. Find the flashcards you need at **www.growthwise.store**.

WANT TO MEET 1-ON-1 WITH JAMES
ABOUT YOUR PERFORMANCE ANXIETY?

Email him at **info@growthwise.us**. Clients typically require two sessions over Zoom.

INTERESTED IN HAVING LIFE-CHANGINGLY GOOD SOCIAL SKILLS?

Consider James' "Make Them Feel Seen" video course or his 1-on-1, 12-week course Social Skills for Life: **www.growthwise.us/socialskills**. Use the code **answertoanxious** at checkout for $20 off "Make Them Feel Seen" or **answertoanxious2** for $100 off "Social Skills for Life."

LOOKING TO OVERCOME ADDICTIVE HABITS OR "STICKY" BEHAVIORS YOU'D LIKE TO ENGAGE IN LESS?

Email James at **info@growthwise.us**. Clients typically require two sessions over Zoom.